Master Your Mind
Champion Your Thoughts

REWIRE YOUR BRAIN

You Have the Ability to Change your Neural Structure
and Rewire your Behaviour, Thoughts & Habits

Harrison S. Mungal, Ph.D, PsyD

Rewire Your Brain

Copyright © 2025 Harrison S. Mungal

All rights reserved. Neither this publication nor any part of this publication may be reproduced or transmitted in any form or by any means, electronic or mechanical, including photocopying, recording or any information storage and retrieval system, without permission in writing from the author.

Contact author
www.agetoage.ca
www.harrisonmungal.com
Facebook: Harrison Mungal
Twitter: HarrisonandKathleen @HKrelationships
AgetoAge @agetoagec
LinkedIn: Harrison Mungal, Ph.D., PsyD
YouTube: Harrison Mungal
Phone: 905-533-1334

ABOUT *the* AUTHOR

Harrison is passionate about life and the people he supports as a therapist with a clinical psychology background. He holds two doctorate degrees, one in Clinical Psychology and the other in Philosophy in Social Work. He has two master's degrees, a master's degree in Social Work and a master's degree in Counselling. And, a Bachelor's degree in Theology. He specializes in mental health, addictions, marriage and relationships, parenting, and the family.

Harrison is considered one of the leading cognitive therapist workshop presenters. He wears many hats in supporting individuals, couples, families, and corporations. He has been a public speaker to over forty-two nations as a keynote speaker at conferences, seminars, and public events, as well as a speaker on several Radio and Television programs. He has written over twenty-five books. He is appreciated for the depth of his knowledge, great humour and passion for relationships, parenting, mental health, addictions, and other related life struggles.

Harrison utilizes a creative scientific-based approach to deliver compelling presentations that have granted him an excellent reputation. He has received several awards and recognitions from local police, mayors, community leaders, managers and directors, and families. He provides training and consultations to various community partners, including psychiatrists, medical doctors, social workers, nurses, police officers, firefighters and senior management teams.

Harrison has been involved in cognitive research to support individuals with addictions, psychosis, anxiety, and depression. He spearheaded several research studies on various themes, including music therapy and schizophrenia, vaccinations for children under six years old, substance abuse and addiction in the food service industry, and Thought Developmental Practice (TDP). His research on TDP with outpatient provided diversion methods to support substance abuse and addictions, anxiety, and depression under the supervision of the chief of psychiatry, Dr. David Koczerginski.

Harrison has over twenty-one years of professional experience working with diverse populations, including seventeen years in mental health and more than ten years as a psychotherapist. These diverse populations include youth and adult offenders, communities impacted by Acquired Brain Injuries, refugees, war victims, and those needing crisis-based support in various settings, i.e., liaison with police, hospitals, community agencies, and inpatient mental health settings.

Harrison specializes in evidence-based therapies, including Cognitive Behavioural Therapy (CBT), Cognitive Processing Therapy (CPT), Dialectical Behavioural Therapy (DBT), Thought Developmental Practice (TDP), Acceptance and Commitment Therapy (ACT), Interpersonal therapy (IPT), Motivational Interviewing Techniques, Grounding Techniques, Integrative Eclectic Therapy, Humanistic Experiential Therapy, Interpersonal Therapy, Supportive Therapy, Exposure Therapy, Visual Therapy, Psychodynamic Therapy.

TABLE Of CONTENT

ABOUT THE AUTHOR 3
INTRODUCTION 7
REWIRE YOUR BRAIN 13
THOUGHT DEVELOPMENTAL PRACTICE (TDP) 31
NEUROGENISIS 39
CONDITION THE MIND 55
MASTER YOUR MIND 69
THE THREE MINDS 79
DEVELOP MENTAL TOUGHNESS 95
THE POWER OF RESILIENCY 107
CHALLENGE IMPULSIVE THOUGHTS 123
CHAMPION YOUR THOUGHTS 141
MASTER YOUR EMOTIONS 157
FEED AND FUEL YOUR BRAIN 177

DEVELOP AND CULTIVATE NEW MEMORIES	193
DEVELOP POSITIVITY	209
CONCLUSION	227
REFERENCES	233

INTRODUCTION

In the fast-paced and ever-evolving world we live in, our minds often become entangled in a web of negativity, self-doubt, and impulsive thoughts. We find ourselves yearning for a way to break free from these patterns and discover the power within us to create a positive and fulfilling life. It is within this context that "*Rewire Your Brain*" emerges as a guiding light, illuminating the path towards mental well-being and a mindset of positivity.

In a world that often feels chaotic and overwhelming, the quest for inner peace and positivity becomes all the more crucial. "*Rewire Your Brain*" stands as a beacon of hope and a transformative guide, offering invaluable insights and practical strategies to help you navigate the labyrinth of your mind. Through the power of neuroplasticity, mental conditioning, and emotional mastery, this book aims to empower you to break free from the grips of negativity and cultivate a mindset that champions your well-being.

Within the intricate framework of your brain, neural pathways are constantly forming, rewiring, and reshaping based on your thoughts, experiences, and actions. This book unveils the awe-inspiring concept of neuroplasticity, illustrating how the brain possesses the remarkable ability to change and adapt throughout your life. By understanding the principles behind neuroplasticity, you gain the keys to unlock your brain's potential, rewiring it for resilience, positivity, and profound personal growth.

"*Rewire Your Brain*" serves as a comprehensive manual, offering a multifaceted approach to master your mind and champion your thoughts. It delves into the depths of mental toughness, teaching you how to rise above challenges and cultivate unwavering resilience in the face of adversity. By challenging impulsive thoughts that hinder your progress, you will uncover the liberating power of intentional thinking, paving the way for personal and professional success.

This book empowers you to become the steward of your own mind, taking charge of your inner dialogue and reshaping it to align with your highest aspirations. By recognizing the profound influence thoughts have on your emotions, behaviours, and overall well-being, you will step into the role of a conscious creator, moulding your reality through the power of positive thinking.

This book is a roadmap, meticulously crafted to empower you in the process of rewiring your brain. It explores the fascinating concept of neuroplasticity, which reveals the brain's incredible ability to change and adapt throughout our lives. By understanding the principles behind neuroplasticity, you will gain the tools necessary to reshape your brain and transcend the limitations imposed by negative thought patterns.

Drawing from the fields of neuroscience, psychology, and personal development, "*Rewire Your Brain*" equips you with practical strategies to condition your mind and cultivate mental toughness. You will delve into the intricacies of developing mental toughness and resilience. You will explore the concept of mental toughness, teaching you how to build resilience and fortitude in the face of adversity. You will uncover strategies to navigate life's challenges with grace and strength, bouncing back from setbacks and adversities.

Through the pages of this book, you will embark on a transformative journey, learning how to challenge impulsive thoughts that hinder your progress and embracing the power of positive thinking. Central to this journey is the idea of championing your thoughts. You will discover the profound impact that your thoughts have on your emotions, behaviours, and overall well-being. With this understanding, you will learn how to master your mind, harnessing the immense potential within you to shape your thoughts consciously and intentionally.

In "*Rewire Your Brain,*" you will explores the power of mastering your emotions, enabling you to respond to life's circumstances in a balanced and mindful manner. By mastering your emotions, you will discover the power to respond to life's challenges with grace and composure, rather than being at the mercy of fleeting impulses and reactive patterns. Within these pages, you will also find guidance on developing positivity and harnessing its incredible benefits. By cultivating a positive mindset, you can transform your life, attract abundance, and create meaningful connections with others.

This book emphasizes the significance of developing and cultivating new memories, enhancing your ability to learn, grow, and adapt. "*Rewire Your Brain*" serves as a comprehensive guide, offering you the tools, knowledge, and inspiration needed to navigate the complexities of the modern world. It is our sincere hope that through the transformative journey outlined within these pages, you will gain the ability to break free from negativity, embrace positivity, and ultimately shape a life filled with purpose, joy, and fulfilment. Let the rewiring begin!

In the depths of our minds lies an untapped reservoir of potential waiting to be unleashed. It is a realm where the forces of neuroplasticity intertwine with our thoughts, emotions, and experiences, shaping the very fabric of our existence. "*Rewire Your Brain*" invites you to embark on an extraordinary voyage of self-discovery and empowerment, as we navigate the intricate pathways of the mind and uncover the secrets to lasting positivity and resilience.

At times, the weight of negativity can cast a shadow over our lives, clouding our judgment and dampening our spirits. The purpose of this book is to help you rise above these challenges, to challenge the impulsive thoughts that hold you back and to forge a new, empowering narrative for yourself. By delving into the fascinating realm of neuroplasticity, we unlock the door to transformation, revealing how the brain can rewire itself, adapting and evolving to support our quest for a more positive and fulfilling existence.

Throughout the pages of "*Rewire Your Brain*," you will encounter a wealth of knowledge and practical tools aimed at conditioning your mind for success.

A profound shift occurs when we develop a deep-rooted positivity within ourselves. "*Rewire Your Brain*" explores the intricacies of cultivating a positive mindset, unveiling the myriad benefits that accompany such a transformation. By rewiring your brain for positivity, you open the door to greater abundance, joy, and harmonious relationships, creating a ripple effect that extends far beyond your own life.

Understanding the power of your mind is essential on this transformative journey. Through an exploration of the Emotional Mind, Reasonable Mind, and Wise Mind, you will gain insight into the intricate workings of your thoughts, emotions, and decision-making processes. By harmonizing these aspects of your mind, you will cultivate a greater sense of self-awareness, emotional intelligence, and wise discernment, guiding you towards balanced and mindful living. Understanding the interplay of the Emotional Mind, Reasonable Mind, and Wise Mind forms a vital aspect of our exploration. These facets of the mind hold immense power and influence over our thoughts, decisions, and actions. By unravelling their dynamics, you will gain valuable insights into your own mental landscape, allowing you to navigate the complexities of life with greater ease and wisdom.

Moreover, "*Rewire Your Brain*" emphasizes the importance of developing and cultivating new memories. Our ability to learn, grow, and adapt hinges on our capacity to create and store new experiences. By tapping into the vast reservoir of your brain's potential, you will harness the ability to shape your memories, forging a tapestry of experiences that enrich your life and propel you forward.

Within the pages of this book, you will find a comprehensive guide, synthesized from the fields of neuroscience, psychology, and personal development. It is a holistic approach, designed to empower you to reclaim your mental landscape and steer it towards a brighter, more positive horizon. By taking this journey, you embark upon a path of self-transformation, where you become the master of your thoughts, the architect of your emotions, and the guardian of your own well-being.

As you immerse yourself in the wisdom contained within these pages, may you find inspiration, guidance, and practical tools to rewire your brain, liberating yourself from the shackles of negativity and embracing the transformative power of positive thinking. Let the journey begin, and may it lead you to a life filled with purpose, resilience, and boundless joy.

Fuelling and nourishing your brain becomes a cornerstone of this journey, as you delve into the profound connection between your mental well-being and the quality of your lifestyle choices. By adopting strategies to feed your brain with nutritious foods, engage in regular exercise, and prioritize self-care, you will lay the foundation for optimal brain function and enhanced cognitive abilities. "*Rewire Your Brain*" recognizes that true transformation encompasses not only the realm of the mind but also the nourishment of the brain itself. We explore the crucial connection between nutrition, exercise, and self-care, unveiling how these elements can fuel and optimize brain function. By adopting habits that prioritize your brain's well-being, you will unlock its full potential, leading to enhanced cognitive abilities, heightened focus, and a profound sense of vitality.

This book is also a guide to developing and cultivating a positive mindset, harnessing its incredible benefits to propel you towards a life of fulfilment and abundance. By shifting your perspective, embracing gratitude, and fostering self-compassion, you will radiate positivity and attract experiences that align with your highest potential. "*Rewire Your Brain*" illuminates the path to self-transformation, where each step forward brings you closer to a life of joy, purpose, and meaningful connections.

Furthermore, "*Rewire Your Brain*" emphasizes the significance of developing and cultivating new memories. The human brain is a remarkable tapestry of experiences, constantly weaving and rewriting its story. By learning techniques to enhance memory formation and retention, you will unlock your brain's potential for continuous growth, deepening your learning capacity, and enriching your life's tapestry with vibrant and meaningful moments.

In the pages that follow, "*Rewire Your Brain*" serves as your steadfast companion on this transformative journey. Drawing upon cutting-edge research, ancient wisdom, and practical exercises, this book offers a comprehensive roadmap to break free from negativity, transcend self-limiting beliefs, and usher in a new era of positivity and empowerment. Together, let us embark on a voyage of self-discovery, rewiring your brain to embrace the boundless possibilities that await you. May this journey empower you to create a life of enduring positivity, resilience, and profound fulfilment.

REWIRE Your BRAIN

Harnessing Neuroplasticity for Personal Growth, we can explore its profound implications for our personal development and mental well-being. Neuroplasticity refers to the brain's remarkable ability to reorganize itself by forming new neural connections and modifying existing ones throughout our lives. It is a fundamental mechanism that allows us to adapt, learn, and grow.

We need to explore various techniques and practices that have been scientifically shown to influence neuroplasticity, enabling us to rewire our brains in ways that promote positive change.

By understanding its fundamental principles, we can appreciate the immense potential it holds for transforming our minds and lives. We need to explore the malleability of the brain and how it continually adapts to our experiences, thoughts, and behaviours.

We need to examine the power of positive thinking and optimism in shaping neuroplasticity to understand the concept of rewiring the brain.

Our thoughts and mindset have a profound impact on the brain, influencing its structure and function. The science behind positive psychology and cultivating an optimistic outlook can enhance neuroplasticity and foster personal growth.

Neuroplasticity is the brain's remarkable ability to adapt, change, and reorganize itself in response to experiences, learning, and environmental stimuli. It refers to the brain's ability to form new neural connections, strengthen existing ones, and even reassign functions to different areas. This concept challenges the long-held belief that the brain is a fixed and unchanging organ.

Neuroplasticity can manifest in two primary ways including structural and functional changes. Structural changes involve alterations in the physical connections between neurons. This can include the growth of new neurons, the formation of new synapses (connections between neurons), or the rewiring of existing connections. Functional changes which involve modifications in the strength and efficiency of existing neural pathways.

Neuroplasticity occurs through various mechanisms, including synaptic plasticity, neurogenesis, and cortical remapping. Synaptic plasticity refers to the ability of synapses to strengthen or weaken based on the frequency and intensity of neural activity. Neurogenesis is the process of generating new neurons, primarily occurring in certain regions of the brain, such as the hippocampus. Cortical remapping refers to the brain's ability to reorganize its sensory and motor maps, such as when a blind person's visual cortex becomes sensitive to touch.

Neuroplasticity is highly influenced by experiences and environmental factors. The brain undergoes changes based on the activities we engage in, the skills we learn, and the information we process. This phenomenon is known as experience-dependent plasticity. For example, learning to play a musical instrument can lead to structural changes in the auditory and motor regions of the brain, enhancing one's musical abilities.

Neuroplasticity is prominent during early brain development, allowing the brain to adapt to its surroundings and establish crucial neural circuits. However, plasticity continues throughout life, albeit to a lesser extent. It plays a role in learning new skills, recovering from injuries, and adapting to changes in the environment. Lifelong plasticity offers hope for individuals with neurological conditions, as it suggests that the brain can compensate for damaged areas by rerouting functions to healthier regions.

Understanding neuroplasticity has profound implications for personal growth and self-improvement. It suggests that our brains are not fixed entities but are malleable and capable of change. By harnessing neuroplasticity, we can actively rewire our brains to develop new habits, acquire new skills, overcome challenges, and promote mental well-being. The subsequent chapters in this book will explore various strategies and techniques to leverage neuroplasticity for personal growth and development.

Neuroplasticity is a fundamental concept that challenges the notion of a fixed brain. It highlights the brain's ability to rewire itself in response to experiences, learning, and environmental factors. Understanding the basics of neuroplasticity provides a foundation for exploring the transformative power of harnessing this phenomenon for personal growth and development.

As we grow older, maintaining cognitive function and mental agility becomes increasingly important. We need to explore the science of aging brains, exploring strategies to support neuroplasticity and preserve cognitive abilities as we navigate the later stages of life.

Through this exploration of neuroplasticity and its various applications, we can aim to empower ourselves with knowledge and practical tools to harness the brain's remarkable capacity for change. By understanding and leveraging neuroplasticity, we create a transformative journey of personal growth and unleash our full potential.

Furthermore, there is a relationship between neuroplasticity and learning. Strategies and techniques enhances memory, knowledge retention, and skill acquisition. From effective study techniques to leveraging spaced repetition and deliberate practice, we can uncover ways to optimize the brain's plasticity to become better learners.

Creativity, a fundamental aspect of human expression, shares a strong connection with neuroplasticity. We should explore how our brain's capacity to rewire itself can unleash our innovative potential. By understanding the neural mechanisms underlying creativity, we can tap into our imagination and unlock new realms of innovative thinking.

In the realm of neuroscience, the concept of neuroplasticity has shed light on our brain's remarkable ability to adapt and rewire itself throughout life. This plasticity extends to learning and memory processes, offering us valuable insights into how we can enhance our cognitive abilities and optimize knowledge retention. By understanding the underlying mechanisms of neuroplasticity, we can develop effective strategies to bolster our learning potential and make the most of our intellectual endeavours.

One key aspect of leveraging neuroplasticity for learning is recognizing the importance of engagement and active participation. Passive learning, such as simply reading or listening to information, can only take us so far. Engaging with the material through practices like active recall and elaboration can only significantly enhance memory formation.

Active recall involves actively retrieving information from our memory rather than passively reviewing it. This practice stimulates our brain to strengthen the neural connections associated with that particular information, making it easier to recall in the future. We have heard of techniques like flashcards, quizzes, or summarizing key concepts in our own words can facilitate active recall and reinforce the neural pathways responsible for encoding and retrieving knowledge. There may be some truths to this.

Elaboration, on the other hand, involves going beyond surface-level understanding and making meaningful connections between our new information and existing knowledge. By linking new concepts to pre-existing mental frameworks, we can create a rich network of associations, which promotes better retention and integration of new information. This strategy encourages the brain to form new synaptic connections and strengthens the neural circuits related to the acquired knowledge.

Another effective strategy for harnessing neuroplasticity in our learning is spaced repetition. Spacing out the review of learned material over time, rather than cramming it all in one session, enhances long-term retention. This approach capitalizes on our brain's ability to consolidate memories through repeated exposure. By spacing out the intervals between review sessions, we engage in a process called memory reconsolidation, in which the brain strengthens and solidifies the memory traces, leading to more durable and accessible knowledge.

Furthermore, incorporating multisensory experiences into our learning process can enhance neuroplasticity. Engaging multiple senses, including sight, sound, touch, and even movement, activates different brain regions and promotes stronger neural connections. Utilizing visual aids, incorporating auditory elements, and engaging in hands-on activities or interactive simulations can all enrich the learning experience and facilitate the formation of diverse neural networks associated with the learned material.

Neuroplasticity is not only limited to cognitive functions such as memory and learning, but it extends to the realm of creativity. Our brain's ability to adapt and change in response to experiences and environmental stimuli provides a fertile ground for nurturing creative thinking.

One way neuroplasticity influences creativity is through the process of divergent thinking. Divergent thinking is the ability to generate multiple solutions, ideas, or possibilities in response to a given prompt or problem. Neuroplasticity enhances divergent thinking by facilitating the formation of new neural pathways and increasing connectivity between different regions of our brains. This increased connectivity allows for the integration of diverse information and the synthesis of ideas from various domains, leading to the emergence of novel and creative solutions.

Furthermore, neuroplasticity plays a role in promoting flexible thinking, which is a crucial aspect of creativity. Flexible thinking involves our ability to shift perspectives, break free from established patterns of thought, and approach problems from different angles.

Neuroplasticity enables our brain to rewire itself, allowing individuals to develop alternative cognitive frameworks and overcome cognitive rigidity. This flexibility in thinking allows for the exploration of unconventional ideas and the ability to connect disparate concepts, fostering creative insights.

Practicing activities that stimulate neuroplasticity can enhance our creativity. Engaging in artistic endeavours including painting, drawing, or playing a musical instrument can activate different regions of our brain and promote the formation of new neural connections. Additionally, engaging in brainstorming sessions, problem-solving activities, and creative exercises can stimulate neuroplasticity by challenging our brain to think in unconventional ways and explore new possibilities.

It is important to note that creativity is not limited to our artistic expression. It permeates various aspects of life, including scientific discovery, technological innovation, and problem-solving in everyday situations. Therefore, nurturing creativity through neuroplasticity has broad implications for personal growth, professional development, and overall well-being.

The relationship between creativity and neuroplasticity highlights our brain's remarkable ability to adapt and rewire itself, opening doors to innovative thinking and problem-solving. By understanding and harnessing neuroplasticity, we can unleash our creative potential, cultivate a flexible mindset, and approach challenges with fresh perspectives. Embracing activities that promote neuroplasticity can foster creativity, leading to personal growth, increased innovation, and a richer and more fulfilling life.

Maintaining cognitive function and mental agility is a significant concern for many of us as we age. Fortunately, neuroplasticity offers a glimmer of hope in this regard. Neuroplasticity remains a powerful mechanism throughout our lives, including during the aging process. By understanding how to harness neuroplasticity, we can potentially enhance cognitive abilities and maintain mental sharpness as we grow older. One approach to promoting neuroplasticity in aging is through cognitive training exercises. These exercises involve challenging our brains with various tasks that target cognitive functions such as memory, attention, and problem-solving. By consistently engaging in these exercises, we can stimulate the brain, prompting it to adapt and rewire itself. This can lead to improved cognitive performance and the preservation of mental abilities.

Neuroplasticity has also proven to be closely linked to learning and memory retention. By implementing effective learning strategies, we have maximized the brain's capacity for rewiring and knowledge acquisition. Through deliberate practice, repetition, and active engagement, we have harnessed neuroplasticity to enhance our learning capabilities and expand our intellectual horizons.

Neuroplasticity has a significant impact on emotional intelligence, which plays a crucial role in our overall well-being and relationships. Emotional intelligence encompasses the ability to recognize and manage our own emotions as well as understand and empathize with others. By understanding how neuroplasticity can enhance emotional intelligence, we can cultivate resilience, improve emotional well-being, and navigate life's challenges more effectively.

Our brains have the remarkable ability to change and adapt throughout our lives, offering hope for developing and strengthening the neural circuits associated with emotional intelligence. With intentional effort, we can rewire our brains to become more emotionally aware, empathetic, and resilient.

Furthermore, creating a supportive and positive environment can foster emotional intelligence through neuroplasticity. Surrounding ourselves with individuals who uplift and inspire us can stimulate the release of oxytocin, a hormone associated with trust and well-being. By fostering healthy relationships and engaging in meaningful connections, we can create a neural environment that supports emotional intelligence.

One way to harness neuroplasticity for emotional intelligence is by practicing positive emotions and cultivating an optimistic mindset. Positive emotions, including joy, gratitude, and love, can shape neural pathways and enhance emotional well-being. By consciously focusing on positive experiences and cultivating an optimistic outlook, we can strengthen the neural connections associated with emotional intelligence.

Developing emotional intelligence requires nurturing self-awareness and empathy. By practicing self-reflection and actively seeking to understand the perspectives and emotions of others, we can strengthen the neural pathways associated with emotional intelligence. This can lead to greater empathy, better communication, and more fulfilling relationships.

Emotional intelligence, a crucial skill for navigating life's challenges, is an area where neuroplasticity plays a vital role. We should explore how emotional intelligence can be developed and enhanced through practices that engage the brain's plasticity. By cultivating self-awareness, empathy, and effective emotion regulation, we can foster resilience and well-being in our personal and professional lives.

Positive thinking and optimism have a significant impact on neuroplasticity, which refers to the brain's ability to rewire itself. Research suggests that cultivating a positive mindset can enhance brain plasticity, leading to numerous benefits for personal growth and well-being.

The process of challenging and modifying negative thought patterns activates neuroplasticity mechanisms in the brain. As we consistently challenge our automatic thoughts, new neural connections form allow for the integration of healthier and more adaptive thoughts and beliefs. Over time, this rewiring of the brain can lead to significant improvements in emotional well-being and behaviour.

Positive thinking also enhances resilience and helps develop effective coping mechanisms. Individuals with an optimistic mindset tend to view challenges or setbacks as temporary and specific rather than permanent and pervasive. This cognitive shift enables them to bounce back from adversity more easily, as they believe in their ability to overcome obstacles and find solutions. By cultivating resilience, we can further promote neuroplasticity and adaptability in the face of life's challenges.

Positive thinking can also facilitate mindset shifts and changes in belief systems. By challenging negative beliefs and adopting a positive mindset, we can rewire our brains to perceive situations differently. This cognitive restructuring promotes the formation of new neural pathways, enabling personal growth and the pursuit of new opportunities.

Cultivating a positive mindset and practicing optimism can have profound effects on neuroplasticity and personal growth. By rewiring the brain through positive thinking, we can enhance resilience, reduce stress, foster creativity, and develop a mindset that promotes adaptability and well-being. Embracing optimism is a powerful tool in harnessing the potential of neuroplasticity for personal growth and a more fulfilling life.

Moreover, positive thinking has been linked to decreased levels of stress and anxiety. Chronic stress can inhibit neuroplasticity, impairing cognitive function and emotional well-being. By adopting an optimistic outlook, we can reduce stress levels and protect our brains from the detrimental effects of prolonged stress. This, in turn, fosters an environment conducive to neuroplasticity and personal growth.

When we adopt an optimistic outlook, our brains form and strengthen neural pathways associated with positive thoughts and emotions. This process reinforces the brain's ability to think positively in the future, creating a self-reinforcing cycle. With repeated positive thinking, these neural pathways become more efficient, facilitating a natural inclination towards positive thoughts.

Optimism encourages a more open and flexible mindset, which is crucial for creativity and problem-solving. By approaching challenges with a positive attitude, we can engage in more divergent thinking, exploring multiple solutions and perspectives. This cognitive flexibility promotes the formation of new neural connections, fostering creativity and innovation.

Mindfulness and meditation have gained significant attention in recent years for their potential benefits in promoting overall well-being and enhancing neuroplasticity. These practices involve cultivating a state of focused attention and awareness of the present moment, without judgment or attachment to thoughts or emotions. By engaging in mindfulness and meditation, we can harness the brain's natural ability to rewire itself, leading to various positive changes in neural structure and function.

Chronic stress can impair neuroplasticity and contribute to various physical and mental health issues. By mitigating the effects of chronic stress, mindfulness and meditation can create a more conducive environment for neuroplasticity to thrive. Mindfulness and Meditation offer powerful techniques for enhancing neuroplasticity and promoting personal growth.

By modulating brain activity, reducing mind-wandering, strengthening cognitive functions, and promoting emotional well-being, these practices can facilitate the rewiring of the brain in positive ways. Incorporating mindfulness and meditation into one's daily routine can provide a foundation for self-discovery, resilience, and the cultivation of a more flexible and adaptable mind.

Furthermore, mindfulness and meditation practices have been found to influence the prefrontal cortex, a region associated with higher-order cognitive functions, emotional regulation, and decision-making. These structural changes suggest an enhancement in cognitive abilities and emotional well-being, as well as improved self-awareness and impulse control.

Moreover, mindfulness and meditation practices promote the cultivation of non-judgmental awareness and acceptance of present-moment experiences, including sensations, thoughts, and emotions. This non-reactive stance allows us to observe our inner experiences without becoming entangled in them. By developing this capacity, we can gain greater control over our thoughts and emotions, which can positively influence neuroplasticity.

Mindfulness and meditation have gained significant attention in recent years. These techniques offer powerful tools for enhancing neuroplasticity. By training our minds to be present and cultivating a state of focused awareness, we can promote structural and functional changes in the brain that support emotional well-being, resilience, and cognitive abilities.

Managing stress and prioritizing mental well-being is crucial for maintaining cognitive function. Chronic stress can negatively impact neuroplasticity and cognitive abilities. Therefore, adopting stress reduction techniques like mindfulness meditation, deep breathing exercises, or engaging in relaxing activities including yoga or tai chi can help mitigate the detrimental effects of stress and support neuroplasticity.

Neuroplasticity remains a powerful ally in maintaining cognitive function and mental agility as we age. By incorporating cognitive training exercises, engaging in regular physical exercise, fostering social connections, consuming a nutritious diet, and managing stress, we can create an environment that supports neuroplasticity and promotes healthy brain aging. With a proactive approach, it is possible to maintain cognitive vitality and enjoy a fulfilling and intellectually stimulating life throughout the aging process.

A vital aspect of maintaining cognitive function and mental agility is the promotion of a healthy lifestyle. Several lifestyle factors have been linked our brain's health in aging. For example, regular physical exercise has been shown to enhance neuroplasticity and preserve cognitive function. Exercise increases blood flow to the brain, promotes the release of beneficial neurochemicals, and supports the growth of new neurons and connections. Engaging in activities including walking, swimming, or dancing can have positive effects on our brain's health and cognitive abilities.

Regular physical exercise is not only beneficial for our physical health but also plays a significant role in enhancing neuroplasticity. Engaging in physical exercise stimulates various physiological processes that can positively impact the brain. When we exercise, our heart rate increases, and blood flow to the brain improves, delivering oxygen and essential nutrients. This increased blood flow promotes the growth of new blood vessels and the release of growth factors that facilitate the development of new neurons and synaptic connections.

One of the key mechanisms through which physical exercise enhances neuroplasticity is the production of neurotrophic factors, which is a protein that supports the survival and growth of neurons, as well as the formation and strengthening of synaptic connections. Physical exercise improves the overall structure and function of the brain, creating a positive effect on our mood and mental well-being. This creates an indirect influence to neuroplasticity.

Exercise releases endorphins, which are natural mood-elevating chemicals in the brain. Regular physical activity can reduce symptoms of depression and anxiety, and improve stress management, all of which can contribute to a healthier brain environment for neuroplasticity to thrive.

It's worth noting that different types of exercise can have varying effects on neuroplasticity. Aerobic exercises, including running and swimming, and resistance training, such as weightlifting or yoga, can promote neuroplastic changes in the brain. Additionally, incorporating variety into our exercise routine can provide additional benefits. Trying new activities challenges the brain to adapt to different movement patterns and motor skills, further stimulating neuroplasticity.

Physical exercise also emerges as a powerful tool for rewiring the brain. Movement and neuroplasticity, explores how different forms of exercise can enhance brain function, boost memory, and promote overall cognitive health. From aerobic activities to strength training and even simple everyday movements, we uncover the transformative effects of physical exercise on the brain.

Overall, physical exercise is a powerful tool for harnessing neuroplasticity and promoting personal growth. By engaging in regular exercise, we can optimize brain health, enhance cognitive function, and support emotional well-being. Whether it's a brisk walk, a yoga class, or a game of tennis, incorporating physical activity into your daily routine can have significant positive effects on your brain's capacity for rewiring and adaptation.

The role of nutrition in brain health cannot be overlooked. We investigate the impact of diet on neuroplasticity, highlighting how certain nutrients and dietary patterns can support optimal brain function and promote neuroplastic changes. We need to explore the connections between gut health, inflammation, and brain health, providing insights into how our food choices can shape our cognitive abilities.

The food we consume plays a vital role in providing the necessary nutrients for optimal brain function, influencing cognitive abilities, memory, and the brain's ability to rewire itself. By adopting a healthy and balanced diet, we can support neuroplasticity and promote our personal growth and well-being.

One crucial aspect of nutrition for neuroplasticity is ensuring an adequate intake of essential nutrients. These include omega-3 fatty acids, antioxidants, vitamins, and minerals, which contribute to the overall health and functioning of the brain. Omega-3 fatty acids, found in abundance in fatty fish like salmon and nuts such as walnuts, are known to support the development and maintenance of brain cells. These healthy fats also assist in reducing inflammation in the brain, which can hinder neuroplasticity.

Antioxidants, which are abundant in fruits and vegetables, play a crucial role in protecting the brain from oxidative stress. Oxidative stress is caused by the accumulation of harmful free radicals, which can damage brain cells and impede neuroplasticity. Consuming a variety of colourful fruits and vegetables, such as berries, spinach, and broccoli, can provide a rich source of antioxidants that support brain health.

Vitamins and minerals are also essential for neuroplasticity. B vitamins, particularly B6, B9 (folate), and B12, are involved in the production of neurotransmitters, which are crucial for communication between our brain's cells. Leafy greens, legumes, and fortified cereals are excellent sources of B vitamins. Additionally, minerals like iron, zinc, and magnesium play essential roles in our brain function and neuroplasticity. Iron-rich foods like lean meats and spinach, zinc-rich foods like oysters and pumpkin seeds, and magnesium-rich foods like dark chocolate and avocados can be incorporated into the diet to support optimal brain health.

It's important to note that a healthy diet for our brain health goes beyond just individual nutrients. Adopting an overall balanced and varied diet is key to ensure that the brain receives a wide range of nutrients for optimal functioning. As we eat a diverse selection of whole foods, including lean proteins, whole grains, fruits, vegetables, and healthy fats, provides a comprehensive nutritional foundation for the brain.

In contrast, diets high in processed foods, saturated fats, refined sugars, and excessive amounts of alcohol can have the opposite effect linking to cognitive decline and impaired neuroplasticity. This type of diets may lead to inflammation, oxidative stress, and an imbalance in neurotransmitters, all of which can negatively impact the brain's ability to rewire and adapt.

A healthy and balanced diet is a valuable tool in optimizing neuroplasticity and supporting personal growth. By incorporating nutrient-dense foods rich in omega-3 fatty acids, antioxidants, vitamins, and minerals, we can provide our brains with the necessary building blocks for optimal functioning and the promotion of neuroplasticity. Additionally, adopting a varied and balanced diet while minimizing processed foods and unhealthy fats can further support brain health and enhance the brain's capacity for growth, learning, and resilience.

The role of our sleep should not be underestimated in the context of neuroplasticity and learning. During our sleep, the brain consolidates and integrates newly acquired information, reinforcing memory traces and enhancing overall cognitive performance. Sufficient quality sleep, is crucial for optimizing neuroplasticity and promoting effective learning. Developing healthy sleep habits, such as maintaining a consistent sleep schedule and creating a conducive sleep environment, can significantly contribute to our improved memory consolidation and retention.

Creativity is a fundamental aspect of human intelligence and has been celebrated throughout history for its ability to inspire innovation and bring forth new ideas. It is the capacity to think in novel and imaginative ways, allowing us to generate unique solutions to problems and make original connections between seemingly unrelated concepts.

Maintaining social connections and engaging in social activities has been associated with better cognitive function in older adults. Social interaction provides mental stimulation, emotional support, and opportunities for learning and intellectual engagement. Participating in social groups, volunteering, or pursuing hobbies that involve interaction with others can contribute to neuroplasticity and overall cognitive well-being.

Finally, we have discovered that neuroplasticity plays a pivotal role in maintaining cognitive function and mental agility as we age. By embracing the principles of neuroplasticity, we have empowered ourselves to defy age-related cognitive decline and preserve our mental acuity. Through lifelong learning, brain exercises, and a holistic approach to brain health, we have nurtured our brains and embraced the possibilities of a vibrant and fulfilling life at any age.

As we conclude this chapter on rewiring the brain, let us celebrate the transformative power of neuroplasticity. We have witnessed first-hand the remarkable ability of our brains to adapt, change, and grow. By embracing the strategies and practices explored throughout this chapter, we have empowered ourselves to unlock our full potential and embark on a journey of personal growth, resilience, and lifelong learning. The power to rewire our brains and create positive change lies within each of us, and with every intentional step we take, we shape a brighter and more fulfilling future.

THOUGHT *developmental* PRACTICE **(TDP)**

Thought Developmental Practice (TDP) developed by Dr. Harrison Mungal has been proven to recondition the mind and restructure thoughts. It creates a diversion to develop new neuropathway in the brain, like teaching the less dominant writing hand to become dominant. Changing negative thinking to become positive, implementing several strategies to help individuals cope.

Thought Developmental Practice (TDP) are widely recognized and effective treatment modality for addiction. It is a structured, time-limited, and goal-oriented psychotherapeutic approach that focuses on identifying, understanding, and changing thinking and behaviour patterns. TDP are grounded in the principle that thoughts, feelings, and behaviours are interconnected, and that altering one can lead to changes in the others. The core concepts of TDP in addiction for example is to identify negative thought patterns. TDP helps individuals recognize and

THOUGHT DEVELOPMENTAL PRACTICE (TDP)

challenge distorted or irrational thoughts that contribute to substance use. It also helps to divert the cravings that comes with the thought pattern. A person might believe that they need a substance to cope with stress, TDP helps to rewire the cravings with several diversion methods.

TDP encourages us to engage in positive behavioural changes by choosing several options to distract the mind when the craving occurs. This might involve learning new coping skills, avoiding triggers that lead to substance use, or practicing healthier lifestyle choices.

TDP equips individuals with skills to manage cravings and avoid relapse. This includes strategies for dealing with stress, regulating emotions, and improving communication skills. TDP helps to recondition the mind with healthy coping strategies which can become a lifestyle.

TDP enhances problem-solving skills, helping individuals to address challenges and setbacks in a more constructive way, reducing the likelihood of turning to substances as a solution.

TDP have been extensively studied and proven effective in treating various substance use disorders. The skills learned through TDP remain with the individual long after the completion of treatment, contributing to long-term recovery.

TDP for addiction is often most effective when integrated with other treatment modalities. This integrative approach acknowledges the complexity of addiction as a disorder that affects individuals on multiple levels – biological, psychological, and social. A key aspect of this integration is the combination of TDP with medication-assisted treatment (MAT). MAT involves the use of medications to manage withdrawal symptoms and reduce cravings, particularly in addictions with a strong physiological component like opioid or alcohol dependence. When MAT is used in conjunction with TDP, the medication helps stabilize the patient's/client's physical symptoms. This allows them to engage more effectively in the exercises to recondition their minds and restructure their thinking with diversion methods. This combination addresses both the neurobiological underpinnings of addiction and the learned behaviours and thought patterns that contribute to the cycle of substance abuse.

Support groups, such as Alcoholics Anonymous (AA) or Narcotics Anonymous (NA), provide another layer of support that complements TDP. These groups offer a community of individuals who share similar experiences and challenges with addiction. The sense of belonging and peer support found in these groups can reinforce the skills and strategies learned in TDP, providing a social context for recovery and an additional layer of accountability.

The integration of TDP with other treatments also extends to addressing co-occurring mental health disorders, such as anxiety or depression. Often, individuals with addiction are also struggling with other psychological issues, which may have contributed to the development of their substance use disorder. Combining TDP with therapies targeted at these co-occurring disorders can provide a more comprehensive treatment approach, addressing all facets of the individual's health.

Personalized treatment plans are essential in this integrative approach. Each person's experience with addiction is unique, and so are their treatment needs. Personalization might involve adjusting the focus and techniques used in TDP, selecting appropriate medications in MAT, and recommending specific types of support groups or additional therapies. This tailored approach ensures that treatment addresses the individual's specific circumstances, challenges, and strengths, increasing the likelihood of successful recovery.

Integrating TDP with other treatments in addiction therapy recognizes the multifaceted nature of addiction and the need for a comprehensive treatment approach. By addressing the biological, psychological, and social aspects of addiction, this integrative approach offers a more holistic path to recovery, tailored to the individual needs of each patient/client.

TDP is highly adaptable, making it an ideal choice for a personalized approach in addiction treatment. The personalization of TDP begins with an understanding that each individual's journey into addiction is unique, influenced by a complex interplay of psychological, environmental, and biological factors. This individualized approach is particularly beneficial because it allows therapists to tailor the therapy to address the specific challenges, needs, and circumstances of each patient/client.

One of the key strengths of TDP in personalization is its flexibility to choose a module or several modules that a patient/client may feel comfortable with. The workbook at hand is meticulously constructed around modules devised to assist individuals dealing with substance abuse, addictions, and pertinent mental disorders. These modules are organized into twelve distinct sections, each replete with practical and stimulating activities.

Contained within TDP are activities expressly selected for their ability to stimulate the brain. The essence lies in the employment of straightforward activities, principles, and concepts systematically arranged to cultivate the mind and reshape thought patterns. It serves as a guide for patients/clients to access and understand their "memory cards," which are often the root causes of anxiety, mood disorders, and addiction issues. It is a tool to bring insight and clarity, enabling individuals to grasp their internal dynamics and interpersonal relationships. The process assists in closing chapters on issues stemming from unresolved past situations and crafting new positive memory cards to replace the old, negative ones.

The ambition of TDP is not to obliterate emotions or the individual's thought process but to enrich coping strategies with practical, uplifting ideas. It seeks to guide individuals in harnessing existing knowledge and behaviours to aid themselves and others. The thrust of TDP is to enable people to unearth the underlying sources of their unhappiness by excavating detrimental habits, thoughts, and ideas and supplanting them with value-driven concepts that instill a sense of self-worth. Exploring causes, effects, and solutions is embarked upon, striving to identify and overcome the emotional and cognitive obstacles impeding progress. For instance, if a patient/client turns to substances as a way of coping with stress, TDP can be directed towards developing healthier stress management techniques. Similarly, for someone whose substance use is linked to social anxiety, the therapy can focus on skills for managing anxiety in social situations.

Moreover, TDP can be adjusted to accommodate the severity of the addiction. For someone in the early stages of addiction, the focus might be on preventing the development of more severe problems. In contrast, for someone with a long history of substance use, TDP might concentrate more on managing cravings and avoiding relapse.

Incorporating personal experiences and preferences is another aspect of personalization in TDP. The therapy sessions can be structured around an individual's life experiences, cultural background, and personal values, ensuring that the therapy resonates more deeply with them. This aspect of personalization is not just about making the patient/client comfortable; it's about enhancing the relevance and effectiveness of the therapy.

TDP's adaptability also extends to its integration with other treatments. For example, in cases where medication is part of the treatment plan, TDP can support medication adherence and address any psychological side effects or misconceptions about medication use. When combined with support groups, TDP's focus on skill development can complement the peer support and shared experiences found in group settings.

Another important aspect of personalization in TDP is the duration and intensity of therapy, which can be adjusted according to the individual's progress and needs. Some may benefit from short-term, intensive TDP, while others may need longer-term therapy to address more deep-rooted issues.

However, TDP is not without challenges too. Challenges and considerations in implementing TDP for addiction are multifaceted, reflecting the complexity of both the treatment modality and the nature of addiction itself. One of the primary challenges in TDP is patient/client engagement and motivation. The effectiveness of TDP heavily relies on the individual's active participation in therapy sessions and their commitment to applying learned strategies outside of these sessions. This can be particularly challenging for individuals struggling with substance use disorders, as factors such as ambivalence about change, fluctuating motivation levels, and the presence of withdrawal symptoms or cravings can impact their ability to fully engage in the therapeutic process.

Another significant consideration is the skill and experience of the therapist. The success of TDP is not solely dependent on the method itself but also on how it is administered. Therapists need to be skilled in establishing a trusting therapeutic relationship, tailoring interventions to meet the unique needs of each patient/client, and adapting the therapy to suit the individual's stage of readiness for change. This requires a deep understanding of the principles of TDP, as well as the ability to be flexible and responsive to the patient's/client's evolving needs.

Moreover, TDP for addiction needs to be sensitive to the complex and often intertwined psychological and emotional issues that accompany substance use disorders. Many individuals with addiction also struggle with co-occurring mental health disorders such as depression, anxiety, or trauma-related disorders. Therefore, TDP must be integrated with treatments addressing these concurrent issues, which adds an additional layer of complexity to therapy.

The therapeutic approach must also consider cultural and socio-economic factors that can influence the patient's/client's experience with addiction and recovery. Cultural sensitivity in TDP involves recognizing and respecting the individual's cultural background and its impact on their perceptions of addiction and treatment. Socio-economic factors like access to resources, social support, and environmental stressors also play a crucial role in both the development of addiction and the recovery process.

Lastly, a critical consideration in TDP for addiction is the maintenance of gains post-treatment. The risk of relapse is a persistent challenge in the treatment of substance use disorders. Ensuring that patients/clients have the necessary support and skills to maintain their recovery after the completion of therapy is essential. This might involve ongoing support groups, booster sessions, or continued engagement in other forms of therapy or self-help programs.

While TDP is a highly effective treatment for addiction, its successful implementation requires careful consideration of patient/client engagement and motivation, therapist expertise, the presence of co-occurring disorders, cultural and socio-economic factors, and strategies for maintaining long-term recovery. Addressing these challenges and considerations is essential for maximizing the effectiveness of TDP in the context of addiction treatment.

THOUGHT DEVELOPMENTAL PRACTICE (TDP)

NEUROGENISIS

Liberating ourselves from the shackles of our past with the focus to live a happy life, we need to create new neuropathy that can dominate our old bad habits, negative behaviours, regrets and emotional wounds. With hearts lighter and minds clearer, we can stand poised on the precipice of a new revelation-the astonishing capacity of our brains to adapt and change. We need to have a better understanding of the brain's ability to adapt and change. We need to embark on a captivating exploration of the profound potential that lies within our neural pathways. It will unveil the extraordinary concept of neuroplasticity, illuminating the brain's remarkable ability to rewire itself, create new connections, and shape our lives in profound ways.

We need to unlock the immense potential of our brains, understanding how we can shape our lives, our relationships, and our futures through the power of adaptive change. We should be prepared by the wonders of neuroplasticity as we uncover the limitless possibilities that lie within each and every one of us.

NEUROGENISIS

Neurogenesis, the process of growing new brain cells, is a captivating phenomenon that reveals the extraordinary regenerative capabilities of the human brain. Once believed that the adult brain was a static entity. Our brains possess the remarkable ability to generate new neurons throughout our lives. This revelation brings with it the promise of a fresh start, a chance for our brains to heal, adapt, and thrive.

At the core of neurogenesis lies the growth and development of neural stem cells, which have the incredible potential to transform into different types of brain cells, including neurons. These neural stem cells reside within specific regions of the brain, such as the hippocampus, a region closely associated with learning, memory, and emotional regulation. Through a precisely orchestrated process, these stem cells undergo divisions, differentiation, and maturation, giving rise to new neurons that integrate seamlessly into the existing neural circuitry.

The implications of neurogenesis extend far beyond the simple addition of new cells. These new-born neurons possess a unique plasticity and adaptability, making them particularly sensitive to environmental stimuli and experiences. As they integrate into the intricate web of neural connections, they contribute to the remodelling and rewiring of neural circuits, allowing for the formation of fresh perspectives and the acquisition of new knowledge.

The significance of neurogenesis for our well-being cannot be overstated. It plays a vital role in various cognitive processes, including learning, memory formation, and pattern recognition. Furthermore, neurogenesis has been closely linked to emotional regulation and mental health, its potential role in reducing anxiety and depression and enhancing overall resilience.

Fortunately, there are practical strategies that can promote neurogenesis and support optimal brain health. Physical exercise, for instance, has been shown to be a potent stimulator of neurogenesis. Engaging in regular aerobic activities, such as jogging, swimming, or cycling, not only improves cardiovascular health but also boosts the production of new neurons in the hippocampus.

A healthy lifestyle that encompasses a balanced diet rich in essential nutrients, sufficient sleep, stress management techniques, and mental stimulation can create an environment conducive to neurogenesis. Certain dietary factors, including omega-3 fatty acids found in fish and antioxidants abundant in fruits and vegetables, have been linked to enhanced neurogenesis and improved brain function.

Engaging in activities that challenge the mind, such as learning a new language, playing a musical instrument, or solving puzzles, stimulates neurogenesis by demanding the brain to form new connections and adapt to novel information. By embracing these strategies and nurturing the growth of new brain cells, we can embark on a journey of self-transformation and personal growth. We have the power to cultivate an environment that supports the rejuvenation of our brains, allowing us to break free from stagnant patterns and embrace the limitless potential for change.

In the depths of our brains, intricate neural networks have formed over the course of our lives, weaving together the fabric of our thoughts, habits, and reactions. These neural networks represent the pathways through which information flows, shaping our perceptions and influencing our behaviours. However, not all of these patterns serve us well. Some are remnants of past experiences, deeply ingrained and often limiting our potential for growth and happiness. It is crucial to recognize the profound influence that these established neural networks have on our lives. They dictate our default responses to situations, determine our automatic thoughts, and even mold our core beliefs. Whether it's a self-defeating belief that we're unworthy of love or a deeply ingrained habit that hinders our progress, these patterns can be pervasive and challenging to overcome.

NEUROGENISIS

Yet, buried within the depths of our neural circuitry lies the promise of change. Neuroplasticity, the brain's remarkable ability to adapt and reorganize itself, offers us the opportunity to rewrite these neural networks and break free from old patterns that no longer serve us.

By observing our thoughts, habits, and reactions, we can identify the neural networks that underlie them. This process of recognition allows us to gain insight into the roots of our patterns and understand how they have shaped our experiences. With this newfound awareness, we can then begin the process of rewiring our brains.

Challenging negative patterns involves actively questioning their validity and replacing them with new, empowering beliefs and behaviours. It requires us to confront the inner critic that reinforces self-doubt and replace its voice with one of self-compassion and encouragement.

One powerful technique for rewiring neural networks is through cognitive restructuring. By consciously examining our thoughts and challenging their accuracy, we can reshape our cognitive landscape. This process involves identifying cognitive distortions, such as all-or-nothing thinking or catastrophizing, and replacing them with more balanced and realistic thoughts.

We need to leverage the power of positive affirmations and visualization. By repeatedly affirming positive beliefs about ourselves and visualizing the desired outcomes, we can create new neural pathways that reinforce empowering behaviours and thoughts. Through repetition and consistency, these new patterns gain strength, gradually replacing the old, limiting ones.

Embracing new experiences and stepping out of our comfort zones plays a crucial role in rewiring our brains. When we engage in novel activities, learn new skills, or expose ourselves to different perspectives, our neural networks adapt and reorganize to accommodate the newfound information. This process of synaptic pruning and strengthening of relevant connections allows us to expand our horizons and forge new paths of thought and behaviour.

It is important to acknowledge that rewiring neural networks is not an overnight process. It requires patience, persistence, and self-compassion. As we challenge old patterns, setbacks may arise, and temporary regression may occur. However, by maintaining a steadfast commitment to our growth and embracing the transformative potential of neuroplasticity, we can gradually break free from the constraints of the past and cultivate new, empowering neural networks that support our pursuit of a happy and fulfilling future.

We need to embark on an exhilarating adventure into the realm of neuroscience, exploring the captivating processes of neurogenesis and neural adaptation. We will unravel the secrets behind breaking free from old patterns and embracing cognitive flexibility, empowering ourselves to navigate the ever-changing currents of life with grace and resilience. Moreover, we need to explore the profound connection between neuroplasticity and emotional well-being, where we could discover how the power of our own minds can heal the wounds of the past and transform trauma into triumph. We need to explore the role of mindfulness, cognitive enhancers, and the social environment in facilitating the rewiring process, offering invaluable tools and insights along the way.

Through the realm of neuroplasticity, remember that the power to recreate your neuropathy lies within you. Let go of any doubts and reservations and open your heart and mind to the remarkable possibilities that await. Say no to the past and embrace the transformative potential of your brain as we embark on this extraordinary adventure together.

The human brain, with its intricate network of billions of neurons, is a marvel of adaptability and change. At the heart of this remarkable capacity lies the concept of neuroplasticity, a phenomenon that has revolutionized our understanding of how the brain functions. Neuroplasticity refers to the brain's extraordinary ability to reorganize itself, forming new neural connections and pathways in response to experiences, thoughts, and emotions.

Consider the example of a person learning to play a musical instrument. At first, the task may feel overwhelming, the notes foreign and the finger movements awkward. However, with practice and repetition, something remarkable occurs within the brain. The neurons responsible for processing the musical information start to form new connections, gradually becoming more adept at coordinating the movements required to play the instrument. Over time, what once felt challenging becomes second nature, as the brain rewires itself to accommodate this newfound skill. This is neuroplasticity in action.

In the ever-changing landscape of life, the ability to adapt and embrace change can become paramount to our personal growth and pursuit of happiness. This is where cognitive flexibility emerges as a powerful tool, enabling us to navigate the twists and turns of our journey with grace and ease. Cognitive flexibility refers to our capacity to shift our thoughts, perspectives, and behaviours in response to new information or circumstances. It empowers us to break free from rigid thinking patterns and open ourselves up to new possibilities, fresh perspectives, and innovative solutions.

Cognitive flexibility is not merely an abstract concept; it plays a pivotal role in shaping our daily experiences and overall well-being. When we are cognitively flexible, we become more adaptable and resilient, capable of responding to unexpected events and embracing change as an opportunity for growth rather than a threat. We are better equipped to navigate through life's challenges, as we possess the ability to adjust our thinking and approach when faced with obstacles or setbacks. By embracing cognitive flexibility, we can invite a sense of freedom and liberation into our lives, allowing us to transcend limitations and unlock new potentials.

One strategy to embrace cognitive flexibility is Reframing. Reframing involves consciously shifting our perspective on a situation or challenge. Instead of viewing obstacles as insurmountable hurdles, we can reframe them as opportunities for growth and learning. By reframing negative experiences into valuable lessons or 'blessings in disguise,' we can transform our thinking and expand our possibilities.

Stepping out of our comfort zones and seeking new experiences is an excellent way to enhance cognitive flexibility. Trying unfamiliar activities, visiting new places, or engaging in creative endeavours can stimulate our brains and encourage us to think in new and unconventional ways. Embracing novelty and embracing the unknown can expand our cognitive repertoire and foster greater flexibility in our thinking.

As we enhance in cognitive flexibility, it is important to remember that change takes time and practice. Be patient and compassionate with yourself as you navigate this process, and celebrate even the smallest moments of growth. By embracing cognitive flexibility, we open ourselves up to a world of possibilities, resilience, and happiness. Let go of rigidity, embrace the power of adaptability, and watch as your life transforms before your very eyes.

Emotional resilience, the ability to adapt and bounce back from adversity, is a fundamental trait that empowers us to face life's challenges with strength and fortitude. There is a fascinating relationship between the brain plasticity and emotional resilience. Unravelling how the remarkable adaptability of our brains can aid us in cultivating emotional well-being is a bonus in understanding the power we carry in our emotions.

At the core of emotional resilience lies the concept of brain plasticity. Our brains possess the remarkable capacity to reorganize, rewire, and form new neural connections throughout our lives. This means that the patterns of thinking, feeling, and responding that once seemed fixed can be reshaped, allowing us to cultivate new emotional responses and adaptive behaviours.

One key aspect of harnessing brain plasticity for emotional resilience is through emotional regulation. By understanding and managing our emotions, we can modulate their intensity and duration, fostering a greater sense of balance and well-being. Techniques such as mindfulness meditation, deep breathing exercises, and journaling can serve as powerful tools in cultivating emotional regulation. These practices enable us to observe and accept our emotions without judgment, empowering us to respond to challenging situations in a more constructive and composed manner.

It is essential to treat ourselves with kindness, understanding, forgiveness and self-compassion. Embracing our imperfections and failures are reflected as self-compassion, which we need to recognize is an inherent part of the human experience. By extending the same compassion and empathy we would offer to a loved one to ourselves, we create a nurturing environment that supports our emotional well-being and resilience.

Positive psychology plays a significant role in harnessing brain plasticity for emotional resilience. This branch of psychology focuses on identifying and fostering strengths, positive emotions, and a sense of purpose and meaning in life. By intentionally cultivating positive emotions such as gratitude, joy, and hope, we can rewire our brains to seek out and amplify these experiences, even in the face of adversity.

Engaging in activities that bring us joy, connecting with loved ones, and practicing gratitude are all powerful ways to promote emotional resilience and rewire our brains towards a more positive outlook. It is important to remember that building emotional resilience through brain plasticity is an ongoing process. Like any skill, it requires practice, patience, and persistence. By consistently engaging in techniques for emotional regulation, embracing self-compassion, and incorporating positive psychology into our daily lives, we gradually reshape our neural pathways, fostering emotional resilience that becomes an inherent part of our being.

In this transformative journey, let us embrace the incredible potential of our brains to adapt and change. By harnessing the power of brain plasticity, we can cultivate emotional resilience, enabling us to navigate life's challenges with grace, strength, and a profound sense of well-being. Together, let us embark on this empowering exploration, rewiring our minds and forging a path toward a future abundant with emotional resilience and happiness.

When our brains encounter traumatic experiences, they respond in ways designed to protect itself in the moment. However, these adaptations can persist long after the threat has passed, leading to a range of emotional, cognitive, and physiological challenges.

Understanding how the brain responds to trauma is a crucial step toward healing and recovery. In the face of overwhelming stress, our brain's alarm system, known as the amygdala, becomes hyperactive, triggering a cascade of responses that prepare us for fight, flight, or freeze. This heightened reactivity can result in a myriad of symptoms, including anxiety, hypervigilance, and emotional numbness.

However, the brain's response to trauma is not limited to the amygdala alone. Other regions, such as the prefrontal cortex, responsible for decision-making and emotional regulation, can be impaired, affecting our ability to cope with distressing memories and emotions. The hippocampus, which plays a vital role in memory formation, may also be impacted, leading to fragmented or distorted recollections of the traumatic event.

Fortunately, the human brain possesses an incredible capacity for healing and recovery. With the right support and interventions, we can move from a place of trauma to a triumphant state of healing and growth. Evidence-based approaches have emerged, shedding light on effective strategies to address and overcome past trauma.

Additionally, somatic practices have gained recognition for their role in trauma recovery. Somatic experiencing, sensorimotor psychotherapy, and other body-oriented therapies recognize the interconnectedness of the mind and body. By engaging the body's wisdom and addressing physical sensations associated with trauma, these practices enable us to release stored tension, regulate our nervous system, and restore a sense of safety and empowerment.

There is an intriguing realm of cognitive enhancers, where science and technology intersect with the pursuit of personal growth. The use of cognitive enhancers, including substances known as nootropics and brain-training exercises, is a powerful tools to enhance neuroplasticity.

Nootropics, commonly referred to as "smart drugs," are substances or compounds that have been shown to enhance cognitive function. These substances range from natural compounds found in plants to synthetic compounds developed in laboratories. Nootropics work by influencing various neurotransmitters, brain chemicals responsible for transmitting signals between neurons. By modulating the activity of these neurotransmitters, nootropics may enhance focus, memory, creativity, and other cognitive abilities.

One of the fascinating aspects of cognitive enhancers is their potential to promote neuroplasticity. As we have learned, neuroplasticity refers to the brain's ability to reorganize itself and form new neural connections. By enhancing neuroplasticity, cognitive enhancers may facilitate the creation of new pathways in the brain, enabling us to acquire new skills, adapt to new situations, and enhance our cognitive abilities.

Brain-training exercises, on the other hand, provide a non-pharmacological approach to cognitive enhancement. These exercises are designed to stimulate specific cognitive functions, such as memory, attention, problem-solving, or language skills. By engaging in targeted mental exercises, we can challenge and stimulate our brains, promoting the growth and strengthening of neural connections.

The potential benefits of cognitive enhancers for personal growth are vast. They offer the tantalizing possibility of accelerating our cognitive development, boosting our productivity, and expanding our mental capabilities. Individuals seeking to improve their performance in academic or professional settings may turn to cognitive enhancers to enhance their focus, memory retention, and overall cognitive agility.

However, it is important to approach the topic of cognitive enhancers with caution and ethical consideration. While some cognitive enhancers have been extensively studied and proven to be safe, others are still in the experimental stages, and their long-term effects remain unclear. Additionally, there are concerns regarding potential side effects, dependency, and the ethical implications of using substances to gain a competitive edge.

Furthermore, it is crucial to recognize that cognitive enhancement is not a substitute for hard work, dedication, and healthy lifestyle choices. Cognitive enhancers should be seen as complementary tools that can support our efforts to maximize our cognitive potential, rather than a shortcut to success. It is essential to maintain a balanced perspective, considering the potential benefits alongside the associated risks and ethical considerations.

As we navigate the realm of cognitive enhancers in the context of brain plasticity, it is important to approach these substances and practices with informed judgment. Understanding the scientific research, consulting with healthcare professionals, and making well-informed decisions are paramount in ensuring our well-being and ethical integrity.

In the pursuit to *"Rewire Your Brain"* from past experiences, cognitive enhancers can serve as valuable allies, augmenting our brain's innate capacity for change and adaptation. By harnessing the potential of cognitive enhancers responsibly and ethically, we can embark on a path of cognitive growth, opening doors to new possibilities and expanding the horizons of our minds.

Our brains are inherently social organs, finely attuned to the nuances of human connection. From the earliest stages of our development, social interactions play a pivotal role in shaping our brains. It is through these interactions that we learn, grow, and adapt to the world around us. The brain, in turn, responds to social stimuli by forging new connections, reinforcing existing ones, and pruning those that are no longer relevant.

Supportive environments act as fertile soil for neural rewiring to flourish. When we find ourselves in environments characterized by positive reinforcement, encouragement, and empathy, our brains respond by creating new neural pathways that facilitate adaptive change. In such nurturing settings, the brain becomes more receptive to learning, open to new ideas, and resilient in the face of challenges.

Equally influential are the social connections we forge throughout our lives. The relationships we cultivate with family, friends, colleagues, and mentors can profoundly impact our neural plasticity. Positive relationships provide a platform for personal growth, as they offer support, validation, and a sense of belonging. Within the embrace of strong social bonds, our brains are primed to adapt, enabling us to navigate life's complexities with greater ease and resilience.

Conversely, negative social influences can impede our brain's ability to rewire itself in positive ways. Toxic relationships, constant criticism, and unsupportive environments can hinder our growth and dampen our neuroplasticity. The neural pathways formed under such circumstances may reinforce negative patterns, restrict our potential, and impede the pursuit of a happy future.

Recognizing the profound impact of social interactions on neural rewiring prompts us to cultivate an environment conducive to growth. Surrounding ourselves with individuals who inspire, challenge, and uplift us can foster adaptive change and propel us toward a happier, more fulfilling existence. Nurturing positive social connections and fostering a supportive network can create a virtuous cycle of growth, amplifying our brain's capacity for rewiring and transformation.

Moreover, our social brain extends beyond face-to-face interactions. In today's interconnected world, digital communities and online relationships also play a significant role in shaping our neural networks. While virtual connections may lack the physicality of in-person interactions, they can still exert a considerable influence on our neuroplasticity. Engaging in online communities that promote positivity, learning, and personal growth can provide a valuable avenue for neural rewiring and self-development.

Embracing the power of supportive environments, nurturing relationships, and positive influences empowers us to shape our neural pathways in ways that propel us toward a future abundant in joy, resilience, and personal fulfilment. By fostering social connections that uplift and inspire, we unlock the potential for transformative change within ourselves and our communities.

Captivating the landscape of neuroplasticity, we inevitably encounter positive change that arises once we have made strides in rewiring our brains. One of the key elements in sustaining positive change is the integration of new behaviours, habits, and thought patterns into our everyday lives. While the initial excitement of transformation may carry us forward, it is the consistency and perseverance in practicing these new ways of being that ultimately solidify the rewiring process. To achieve this, it is important to develop a comprehensive plan for integrating these changes into our routines.

It is crucial to establish clear and specific goals that align with the positive changes we may seek to sustain. By defining these goals, we can create a roadmap that guides our actions and provides a sense of purpose. We need to break down these goals into manageable steps, setting realistic expectations and timelines. This helps to ensure that the changes we make are both sustainable and attainable.

Incorporating new behaviours and habits into our daily life requires commitment and practice. Consistency is key. We need to set aside dedicated time each day to engage in the activities that support our positive changes. Whether it is practicing mindfulness, engaging in physical exercise, or journaling, make it a non-negotiable part of our routine. Over time, these intentional actions will become ingrained in our neural pathways, solidifying the rewiring process.

Additionally, it can be beneficial to create visual reminders or cues that prompt us to engage in our desired behaviours. This can be as simple as placing sticky notes with positive affirmations around our living space, using technology to set reminders on our phone, or creating a vision board that visually represents our goals and aspirations. These visual cues serve as constant reminders and reinforcement of our commitment to sustaining positive change.

It is important to acknowledge that setbacks and challenges may arise along the way. Embrace these as learning opportunities rather than moments of failure. When faced with obstacles, reflect on what triggered them and explore alternative strategies to overcome them. Cultivate self-compassion, recognizing that change takes time and effort. Be patient with yourself and celebrate even the smallest victories, for they are all milestones on your path to lasting positive change.

Practicing self-care is paramount in sustaining positive change. We need to nurture our physical, mental, spiritual and emotional well-being through activities that replenish and rejuvenate us. Prioritize sleep, engage in activities that bring us joy, and cultivate a positive mindset.

When we take care of ourselves holistically, we create a solid foundation upon which positive changes can flourish and endure.

Rewriting neural networks has been a pivotal step in breaking free from old patterns that no longer serve us. We have harnessed the power of cognitive flexibility, adapting to change with ease and grace. Through intentional effort and practice, we have reshaped our thinking patterns and behaviours, allowing for new pathways to form and old limitations to dissolve.

Embracing cognitive flexibility has not only enhanced our ability to adapt to change but has also strengthened our emotional resilience. By harnessing brain plasticity for emotional well-being, we have developed the capacity to navigate challenges and bounce back from adversity with greater ease. Our minds have become more agile and adaptable, enabling us to maintain a positive outlook even in the face of difficulties.

The social brain has also played a significant role in our neural rewiring journey. We have recognized the influence of our social environment on our brain's ability to adapt and change. By surrounding ourselves with positive influences and nurturing supportive relationships, we have created an environment that fosters growth, learning, and neural rewiring.

As we conclude this chapter, let us celebrate the progress we have made in recreating new neuropathy. We have witnessed firsthand the incredible capabilities of our brains to adapt, heal, and transform. Through the principles and practices explored in this chapter, we have embraced the power of neuroplasticity to create positive and lasting change in our lives.

Moving forward, let us sustain this positive change by incorporating the strategies for long-term success that we have discovered. By nurturing our brain's plasticity through continued learning, mindfulness, and self-care, we can ensure that our journey of growth and transformation remains vibrant and ongoing.

NEUROGENISIS

As we embark on the next chapter of our lives, let us carry with us the knowledge that we have the power to recreate and reshape our neuropathy. With each intentional step we take, our brains are primed for growth, adaptation, and the creation of a life filled with fulfilment, resilience, and boundless possibilities.

CONDITION *The* MIND

In this fast-paced and often challenging world, maintaining a positive outlook can be an invaluable asset. It not only enhances our overall well-being but also empowers us to navigate life's ups and downs with resilience and grace. There is profound influence of conditioning the mind to stay positive and optimistic to *"Rewire Your Brain."*

The power of a positive mindset is undeniable. It shapes our perceptions, influences our emotions, and fuels our actions. When we embrace positivity, we open ourselves to a world of possibilities, where obstacles become opportunities and setbacks transform into steppingstones towards personal growth and success. However, maintaining such a mindset requires conscious effort and a commitment to self-improvement.

We need to explore the science behind conditioning the mind for positivity, understanding how our thoughts and beliefs can be rewired to create a more optimistic outlook on life. We need to explore practical techniques and strategies that can help us challenge and reframe negative thoughts, develop gratitude as a daily practice, and embrace failure as an essential part of the journey towards success.

Additionally, we need to explore the significance of positive self-talk, discovering how the way we speak to ourselves can shape our reality. By cultivating a supportive and encouraging inner dialogue, we can uplift our spirits, boost our confidence, and foster a deep sense of self-belief.

Finding joy in the present moment is a crucial aspect we need to explore. Often, our minds wander between regrets of the past and anxieties about the future, causing us to miss the beauty and opportunities available right now. By practicing mindfulness and embracing the present, we can cultivate a greater appreciation for life's small pleasures and experiences.

Furthermore, we need to explore the importance of engaging in activities that bring us genuine happiness and fulfillment. Nurturing our passions and prioritizing self-care not only rejuvenates our spirits but also strengthens our overall well-being. Also, the power of forgiveness and letting go, understanding how releasing past resentments can free us from emotional burdens and enable us to move forward with a lighter heart.

Embracing optimism as a way of life need to be a central theme in our lives to reduce stress and anxiety and allow the past to float away from our present to *"Rewire Your Brain."*

Adopting an optimistic mindset can have a positive impact on our lives, relationships, and overall happiness. By shifting our perspective and focusing on the possibilities and potential inherent in every situation, we can create a life infused with hope, resilience, and a deep appreciation for the journey.

Sustaining a positive mindset requires consistent practice. We need practical tips and strategies to incorporate into our daily routines, ensuring that positivity becomes a habit rather than a fleeting state of mind. By nurturing our minds and conditioning ourselves to stay positive, we can lay the foundation for a lifetime of happiness and fulfillment.

A positive mindset is a powerful tool that can significantly impact our lives and the way we experience the world. It is the foundation upon which we build our thoughts, emotions, and actions, shaping our perceptions and influencing our overall well-being. Understanding the power of a positive mindset requires recognizing its profound effects on various aspects of our lives. It will enable us to approach challenges and obstacles with resilience and optimism. Instead of being overwhelmed by difficulties, we will view them as opportunities for growth and learning. It is our ability to find solutions and persevere, which increases our chances of overcoming obstacles and achieving success.

Moreover, a positive mindset enhances our emotional well-being. When we adopt a positive outlook, we tend to experience more positive emotions such as joy, gratitude, and contentment. These positive emotions have a ripple effect, influencing our overall mood, and improving our mental and emotional state. By focusing on the positive aspects of our lives, we can counteract negative emotions and cultivate a sense of well-being.

A positive mindset enhances our relationships and social interactions. When we approach others with positivity, we radiate warmth and kindness, creating a positive environment that fosters deeper connections. Our positive attitude attracts like-minded individuals and strengthens existing relationships. By maintaining an optimistic perspective, we can build and nurture meaningful connections that enrich our lives.

CONDITION THE MIND

Furthermore, a positive mindset can improve our physical health. It can have a positive impact on our immune system, cardiovascular health, and overall well-being. When we maintain a positive mindset, we are more likely to engage in healthy behaviours such as regular exercise, a balanced diet, and adequate rest, all of which contribute to better physical health.

Additionally, a positive mindset opens us up to a world of possibilities. When we believe in ourselves and our abilities, we are more willing to take risks, explore new opportunities, and step outside our comfort zones. This mindset encourages us to embrace change, seize opportunities, and pursue our goals and dreams with enthusiasm and determination. By cultivating a positive mindset, we expand our horizons and create a life that is fulfilling and aligned with our aspirations.

Understanding the power of a positive mindset requires acknowledging that it is not about denying or ignoring the challenges and hardships of life. Instead, it is about choosing to focus on the positive aspects, finding meaning in adversity, and responding to difficulties with resilience and optimism. A positive mindset empowers us to shape our reality and create a life that is filled with happiness, fulfillment, and a deep appreciation for the present moment.

The science behind conditioning the mind for positivity is rooted in the fields of neuroscience, psychology, and cognitive behavioural therapy. These disciplines provide valuable insights into how our thoughts, emotions, and behaviours are interconnected, offering a framework for understanding and harnessing the power of a positive mindset.

One key aspect of conditioning the mind for positivity is challenging and reframing negative thoughts. Our minds have a natural tendency to focus on negative experiences or anticipate negative outcomes, which can lead to a pessimistic outlook. However, through techniques such as cognitive restructuring, we can challenge the accuracy and validity of negative thoughts and replace them with more positive and realistic alternatives. This process involves examining the evidence for and against negative beliefs, identifying cognitive distortions, and consciously choosing thoughts that are more empowering and uplifting.

Embracing failure as a steppingstone to success is an integral part of conditioning the mind for positivity. Often, we perceive failure as a personal flaw or a permanent setback, which can hinder our growth and resilience. However, by reframing failure as a valuable learning opportunity and a natural part of the journey towards success, we can overcome fear and develop a more optimistic mindset. Research indicates that we who view failure as a temporary setback and maintain a positive outlook are more likely to persevere and achieve our goals.

Positive self-talk plays a crucial role in conditioning the mind for positivity. The way we speak to ourselves can significantly impact our emotions, beliefs, and behaviours. By consciously replacing self-criticism and negative self-talk with supportive, compassionate, and empowering language, we can foster a positive self-image and cultivate greater self-confidence. The science of self-affirmation demonstrates that positive self-talk can reduce stress, boost motivation, and improve performance in various domains of life.

Moreover, engaging in activities that bring us happiness and fulfillment has a profound effect on our overall well-being. When we participate in enjoyable and meaningful experiences, our brains release neurotransmitters like dopamine and endorphins, which are associated with feelings of pleasure and happiness. Regular engagement in such activities not only enhances our mood but also contributes to a positive mindset by reinforcing the belief that we are deserving of joy and fulfillment.

Overall, the science behind conditioning the mind for positivity provides us with a deeper understanding of how our thoughts, emotions, and behaviours influence one another. By utilizing techniques rooted in neuroscience, psychology, and cognitive behavioural therapy, we can rewire our thinking patterns, cultivate gratitude, embrace failure, practice positive self-talk, and engage in activities that promote happiness. Through consistent effort and practice, we can condition our minds to stay positive and optimistic, leading to greater well-being, resilience, and a more fulfilling life.

Our thoughts have a profound impact on our emotions, behaviours, and overall well-being. Negative thoughts can weigh us down, create self-doubt, and limit our potential. However, by learning to challenge and reframe negative thoughts, we can regain control over our mindset and cultivate a more positive and optimistic outlook on life.

The first step in challenging negative thoughts is to become aware of them. Often, negative thoughts can become automatic and ingrained in our thinking patterns, making it difficult to recognize their presence. We need to condition our minds to become mindfulness and self-reflected in this process. By observing our thoughts without judgment, we can start identifying negative thinking patterns and their triggers.

Once we have identified negative thoughts, the next step is to examine their validity and challenge their accuracy. Often, negative thoughts are distorted or exaggerated, creating an inaccurate perception of reality. This is where rational thinking comes into play. We can ask ourselves questions such as: 'Is there concrete evidence to support this negative thought?" "Are there alternative explanations or perspectives?" "What would a trusted friend or mentor say about this thought?"

By critically evaluating our negative thoughts, we can begin to dismantle their power over us. We can replace irrational or exaggerated beliefs with more balanced and realistic ones.

Reframing negative thoughts involves consciously shifting our perspective and finding alternative, more positive interpretations. For example, if we catch ourselves thinking, "I always mess things up," we can reframe it as, "I've made mistakes in the past, but I'm constantly learning and growing. Mistakes are opportunities for improvement."

Another powerful technique is to replace negative self-talk with self-compassion. Instead of berating ourselves for perceived failures or shortcomings, we can offer ourselves understanding, kindness, and support. Treating ourselves with the same compassion we would extend to a loved one allows us to challenge negative thoughts and replace them with self-empowering affirmations.

Moreover, challenging and reframing negative thoughts involves seeking evidence that contradicts the negativity. When we find ourselves entertaining thoughts like, "I'm not good enough," we can intentionally recall past accomplishments, compliments from others, or moments of success. This practice helps counterbalance negative self-perceptions and reinforces a more positive self-image.

It's important to note that challenging and reframing negative thoughts is an ongoing process that requires practice and patience. It may not happen overnight, but we can condition our minds with consistent effort, we can gradually reshape our thinking patterns and develop a more optimistic mindset.

Challenging and reframing negative thoughts is a powerful tool for cultivating a positive and optimistic mindset. By becoming aware of our negative thoughts, examining their validity, and replacing them with more balanced and positive alternatives, we can transform our outlook on life. With practice and persistence, we can break free from the limitations imposed by negative thinking and embrace a mindset that empowers us to thrive and find joy in every aspect of our lives.

In a world filled with distractions, challenges, and uncertainties, cultivating a sense of gratitude can be a transformative practice that brings joy, contentment, and perspective into our lives. Gratitude allows us to shift our focus from what may be lacking or going wrong to what is abundant and going right. It encourages us to appreciate the present moment and recognize the blessings that surround us, no matter how big or small.

In addition to these intentional practices, we need to condition our minds to cultivate a mindset of gratitude throughout the day. Pay attention to the small moments and experiences that often go unnoticed. Take a pause to savour a delicious meal, admire the beauty of nature, or relish in the warmth of a hug. By being fully present and appreciating these moments, you infuse your daily life with gratitude and develop a deeper sense of fulfillment.

Challenging times and difficult circumstances can make it challenging to find gratitude. However, it is during these moments that gratitude becomes even more crucial. By reframing challenges as opportunities for growth, we can find hidden blessings and valuable lessons within them. Embracing a mindset that seeks gratitude even in adversity allows us to cultivate resilience and inner strength.

It's worth noting that developing gratitude as a daily practice requires consistency and commitment. Like any habit, it takes time and effort to integrate gratitude into our lives fully. Start with small, achievable steps and gradually increase the frequency and depth of your gratitude practice. Over time, you will find that gratitude becomes a natural and integral part of your daily life.

Developing gratitude as a daily practice is a powerful way to enhance our well-being and foster a positive mindset. By intentionally focusing on the blessings in our lives, expressing appreciation to others, and maintaining a mindset of gratitude, we can cultivate a deeper sense of contentment, joy, and resilience.

We need to condition our minds that finding joy in the present moment is a beautiful practice that allows us to fully immerse ourselves in the richness of life. It involves cultivating awareness, embracing our surroundings, and savoring the simple pleasures that often go unnoticed.

By shifting our focus to the present, we can break free from the constraints of the past and the worries of the future, experiencing a profound sense of contentment and fulfillment.

One way to find joy in the present moment is by engaging our senses. Our senses connect us with the world around us, and by consciously tuning into them, we can deepen our experience of the present. Take a moment to notice the vibrant colours of nature, the soothing sounds of birds chirping or waves crashing, the gentle touch of a loved one's hand, or the tantalizing aroma of freshly brewed coffee. By savouring these sensory experiences, we can elevate our enjoyment and create a deeper connection with the present moment.

Cultivating a childlike sense of curiosity allows us to approach each moment with fresh eyes and an open mind. Conditioning our minds to embrace a mindset of exploration, seeking out new experiences, and finding joy in the simple wonders of everyday life. Whether it's trying a new hobby, exploring a new neighbourhood, or learning about a new topic, approaching life with a sense of curiosity can infuse our days with a sense of excitement and discovery.

Engaging in activities that bring us joy is essential for finding happiness in the present moment. Each person has unique passions and interests that ignite their soul. It could be painting, dancing, playing an instrument, gardening, or any other activity that brings a deep sense of fulfillment. By carving out time for these activities and fully immersing ourselves in them, we create moments of pure joy and lose ourselves in the flow of the present.

Connecting with others is a powerful way to find joy in the present moment. Human connection has a profound impact on our well-being and sharing meaningful moments with loved ones can bring immense happiness. Whether it's engaging in heartfelt conversations, sharing laughter, or simply enjoying each other's company, nurturing our

CONDITION THE MIND

relationships allows us to create memories and experience the joy of being present with those we care about.

We need to condition our minds to find joy in the present moment that can be as simple as slowing down and appreciating the beauty of the here and now. In our fast-paced lives, we often rush through our days, missing out on the small moments of joy that are scattered throughout. By intentionally slowing down, we can cultivate a sense of presence and mindfulness, allowing us to truly appreciate the beauty in the mundane. It could be relishing a quiet moment with a cup of tea, watching the sunset, or taking a leisurely stroll in nature. These moments of pause and reflection enable us to fully embrace the present and find joy in its simplicity.

Incorporating these practices into our daily lives can transform our relationship with the present moment. By engaging our senses, cultivating curiosity, pursuing activities that bring us joy, connecting with others, and slowing down, we open ourselves to a world of vibrant experiences and profound fulfillment. The present moment holds infinite possibilities for joy, and by embracing it wholeheartedly, we can create a life filled with richness, gratitude, and unending happiness.

In our pursuit of positivity and optimism, it is vital to actively seek out and engage in activities that bring us genuine happiness. These activities serve as powerful catalysts, rejuvenating our spirits, and fostering a sense of fulfillment in our lives. By intentionally carving out time for the things that bring us joy, we create an environment that nurtures our well-being and uplifts our overall outlook.

The beauty of engaging in activities that bring us happiness lies in their personal and subjective nature. What brings joy to one person may differ from another, and that's perfectly okay. The key is to explore and identify the pursuits and experiences that resonate with us on a deep level, igniting a sense of passion and contentment within.

It could be as simple as reconnecting with a childhood hobby that has always brought us joy, such as painting, playing a musical instrument, or gardening. Engaging in these activities allows us to tap into a state of flow, where time seems to dissolve, and we immerse ourselves completely in the present moment. The creative process can be deeply therapeutic, providing a sense of accomplishment and serenity.

For some, physical activity is a gateway to happiness. Engaging in sports, yoga, dancing, or any form of exercise not only benefits our physical well-being but also releases endorphins, commonly known as "feel-good" hormones. The exhilaration of movement and the sense of vitality that accompanies it can significantly contribute to our overall mood and outlook on life.

Exploring the great outdoors can also be a source of immense joy and tranquility. Whether it's hiking in nature, taking a leisurely stroll along the beach, or simply spending time in a local park, immersing ourselves in natural surroundings has a profound impact on our well-being. The beauty and serenity of the natural world have a way of grounding us, instilling a sense of peace and appreciation for the wonders of life.

Engaging in activities that involve connection and social interaction can be particularly uplifting. Spending quality time with loved ones, friends, or participating in group activities that align with our interests can foster a sense of belonging and fulfillment. Engaging in meaningful conversations, sharing laughter, and creating cherished memories with others enhances our sense of social connection, which is a fundamental aspect of human happiness.

Moreover, acts of service and giving back to the community can also bring a deep sense of joy and purpose. Volunteering for a cause that resonates with our values allows us to contribute to something greater than ourselves. The act of helping others not only positively impacts their lives but also fills our hearts with gratitude and a profound sense of fulfillment.

Ultimately, engaging in activities that bring us happiness is an invitation to prioritize self-care and cultivate a life that is aligned with our authentic selves. By consciously making time for these pursuits, we honor our individuality and prioritize our own well-being. In doing so, we create a positive feedback loop, where our happiness and optimism fuel our actions, and in turn, our actions nurture our happiness and optimism.

We need to condition out minds that optimism is not merely a fleeting emotion or a temporary state of mind; it is a way of life. When we embrace optimism, we choose to view the world through a lens of hope, resilience, and possibility. It is a conscious decision to focus on the potential inherent in every situation and to approach challenges with a positive and proactive mindset.

Achieving a positive mindset is not a one-time accomplishment; it requires ongoing effort and commitment. By integrating positive habits into our daily routines, we can reinforce our mindset, fortify our resilience, and experience lasting happiness.

Consistency is key when it comes to cultivating a positive mindset. Just as physical exercise strengthens our muscles over time, consistently practicing positive habits strengthens our mental and emotional well-being. By making positivity a priority in our lives, we create a ripple effect that permeates all aspects of our being, influencing our thoughts, emotions, and actions.

One way to sustain a positive mindset is through the regular practice of practicing positive habits. Expressing a positive mindset for the blessings, big and small, in our lives helps us shift our focus from what may be lacking to what we have already received. By setting aside time each day to reflect on and appreciate the positive aspects of our lives, we foster a sense of abundance and contentment.

Our inner dialogue has a significant impact on our thoughts, beliefs, and overall outlook on life. Consistently speaking to ourselves with kindness, encouragement, and compassion helps build a strong foundation of self-belief and self-worth. When we catch ourselves engaging in negative self-talk, we can consciously reframe those thoughts into positive affirmations, empowering ourselves and shifting our mindset towards optimism.

Additionally, sustaining a positive mindset involves consciously challenging and reframing negative thoughts. Negative thoughts can often sneak into our minds, undermining our confidence and dampening our optimism. By consistently practicing self-awareness, we can identify negative thoughts as they arise and consciously choose to challenge their validity. We can reframe them by replacing negative beliefs with more positive and empowering perspectives.

The people we interact with and the environments we immerse ourselves in can greatly impact our overall outlook on life. By consciously choosing to surround ourselves with individuals who radiate positivity and who support our growth, we create a nurturing ecosystem that reinforces our commitment to maintaining a positive mindset.

Consistent practice entails staying committed to personal growth and self-improvement. It involves being open to learning, adapting, and embracing new perspectives. By consistently seeking opportunities for growth, whether through reading, attending workshops, or seeking guidance from mentors, we expand our knowledge and nurture a mindset that is receptive to change and personal development.

Letting go of past resentments and forgiving others has been a liberating experience. We have realized that holding onto grudges only weighs us down and prevents us from experiencing true happiness and peace. By practicing forgiveness, we have released the burdens of the past and created space for healing, growth, and positive connections.

CONDITION THE MIND

As we conclude this chapter, let us celebrate the transformative journey we have embarked upon to condition our minds for positivity and optimism. With consistent practice, determination, and a belief in our own potential, we can say goodbye to our past and "*Rewire Your Brain.*"

MASTER Your MIND

The mind is the most powerful gift we were created with, along with the heart, and if we don't use our minds correctly, it can be highly destructive. The thoughts that flow through our minds can either be a blessing or a curse. The thoughts we entertain affect our perception and how we interpret information. We all struggle from time to time with our complex thinking patterns, however, with the help of divergent thinking, we can set our minds free.

We need to let our thoughts flow smoothly but should not allow them to rule us. Our thoughts can run wildly if we do not take control of them. Controlling our thoughts is like raising children. If we don't master parenting, our children will walk all over us. They will then bring shame and disrespect upon themselves and their families. Similarly, lacking control over the mind will bring negative consequences. Unwanted thoughts that reside in our mind, will create unproductive and unhealthy thinking. Changing our thinking to dispel such thoughts will eventually allow us to control our behaviours.

Mastering the mind involves managing the thoughts that flow through the mind. It involves reprogramming our thinking. This takes skill and like any talent must be developed. Mastering the mind is like mastering a career or hobby, except the mind is with us twenty-four-seven.

Learning a language takes time, regardless of who we are and what culture or ethic background we are from. The speak a language with the perfect dialect takes a lot of effort and experience speaking. Similarly, we can master our minds with the same principles. The more effort we give, the less stressful we will be in the process. Everything in life takes time to master like a language. The more we practice speaking it the more fluent it becomes.

When we master our thinking we can actually change our feelings which will enable a greater level of peace in our thought life. We can do two main things to take control of our minds; we can either replace our thinking with new thoughts or we can interrupt our thinking. Both require us to become more aware of impulsivity in our thoughts. When we master our minds, we will finally learn to control our thinking.

There are many thoughts that take up a lot of space in our brains. Like "squatters," who do not have permission to live in the location they chose. Some of our thoughts are there in our minds not because we have consciously given permission, but they came along as a result of past hurts. The more they are fed with negativity they more controls they have and eventually they rule the mind just like a squatter who will take over land or a residence they reside in. In order to take charge, make sure you are the one consciously permitting these thoughts to stay in your mind, otherwise, dispel them.

There is usually a loose conglomeration of thoughts running through our minds that come from words that were spoken to us as children. It is often the case that these words take up space in our minds. These are usually thoughts that have us comparing ourselves with others, believing that we are useless, feeling that we will never succeed, or constantly in a state of trying to fulfill other people's expectations of us. The conglomeration of thoughts that come from rejection and betrayal which creates emotional pain should be discarded ceremoniously like putting an object that represents negativity in a box and burying or burning it. These are the thoughts that cripple us and instead of being a master over our minds, we become a slave to them.

We should never allow our thoughts to make us feel like we are in bondage or like we are a slave to fear and worry. Anger, frustration, emotional pain, and regrets grow when we live in bondage. A lack of motivation, low self-esteem, insecurity, anxiety, depression, passivity, and violent behaviours are all signs that we may be in bondage due to our thoughts. Despite how much effect our thoughts can have on us, we are the masters of what we think. We need to stop ourselves from thinking negatively. Start by saying to yourself " I am in control." We can actually write it down or print on it paper "I am in control" and paste it in places where it is visible to remind ourselves we are in charge of ourselves. We should not be blaming others for our behaviours and actions.

Another behaviour we should avoid is beating up on ourselves. It is okay to admit our flaws and faults and move on. Don't allow thoughts of self-disappointment to stay in your brain. No one can change what has happened, however, we can problem-solve. Therefore, looking for solutions instead of allowing negative thoughts to rule our minds should be our focus when things do not go the way we want them to. Sometimes we are our worst bullies. Don't allow your mind to bully you with negative thoughts.

Some unanswered questions that may help you that is usually asked. "What are some tricks and pointers to becoming masters of your minds?" "How do we get rid of the slave mentality?" "How do we take charge of our thinking?"

Most of us need to change our attitude toward ourselves and others at least at some point in our lives. We need to come to a place in life where we can conclude we don't have all the answers to all of life's problems and we cannot "fix" others who may have wronged us. Let that new positive attitude extend even to our enemies. When we start living in this fashion, we will grasp the basics of mastering our mind.

We should be alert to opportunities, realizing that opportunities may never come by again and take advantage of them when they are in your hands. We may fail, but that's a risk we will have to take. Each failure will draw us closer to the prize. Opportunities will expand our experience and develop our skill set.

We need to accept people for who they are instead of trying to change them to be us. We all do our own assessment of people we meet and make a conscious decision to engage with them or maintain a distance. Accepting the fact that we cannot change anyone but we can work with them is another skill we need in order to master the mind. We can give suggestions and recommendations but cannot make someone become the person we want. A great deal of anxiety comes from feeling a lack of control when people do not behave how we want them to. People may even do things that can negatively influence us. Learning to accept others while being yourself and to let them make their own choices will have a positive impact on your relationship with them which in turn will positively impact your outlook.

When we take responsibility, we set a different paste in life. We create a blue print for others to follow. Regardless of what issues may arise as a result of our participation, we need learn to take responsibility. We could be 100% right or 100% wrong, we should take responsibility in finding a solution rather than blaming others. This shows maturity but it is also a trick to allowing ourselves to learn that we are a master of our lives. So many of us live our lives more or less by ourselves and fail to include others. We need to ask ourselves why? Where did it stem from? We can socialize and engage with others and not allow the power of influence to affect us. We can be in control of our mind, what we think of ourselves and others without allowing fear to control us. We were created to be among others to help with healthy stimulants, which assist with preventative factors that will affect our mental health long term.

We need to maintain a mind of a student. Some of us may give the impression that we know it all and that we have an answer for everything in life, yet our own lives are falling apart. It is only to compensate for self-perceived or actual incompetence. We can learn on a daily basis from other people around us. We may learn minor things or get major revelations, but when we are willing to learn, we will always be one step closer to master what we are learning. Assuming the role of a student allows for new thoughts to replace discarded thoughts as we stay in control of what we allow into our minds.

We also need to maintain a mind of a teacher. One thing observed from teaching is that it forces you to learn. When time is spent preparing a lesson, knowledge is gained. And, when we teach, experience and skills are sharpened. Being a teacher sometimes forces us to take control of what we are saying and how we are saying it to ensure that others receive our message effectively. Find out how we can speak into the lives of others even if it's our love ones. The concept of centering our thoughts around communicating a theme will help us in taking control of our thought life.

When the brain is "infected," things can go awry, and the brain no longer serves its purpose efficiently. Symptoms of thought disorders will result as the brain can no longer "carry a conversation" that is sensible. Our brain is a miracle how it function as it holds more information than we could ever imagine. It houses resources we can tap into in the future in an orderly fashion which enables us to perform various impressive tasks. Think of the first time you tried riding a bike. Your brain needed to recall many thoughts in order to keep the bike upright, and it does not matter how many years later you will still know how to ride a bike.

We can become great servants to our minds if we fail to become masters over it. We may find ourselves feeling we cannot control what we think, do or say, but it is possible with proper discipline. Spend time concentrating and thinking through your thoughts before acting, forming opinions, or communicating opinions. We need to learn how to filter our thoughts if we want to master them.

Mastering our minds draws us closer to the destinies assigned to us. We need to come to a place where we can master our minds, otherwise we will never be at peace with ourselves. We need to control what goes into our mind. If it's not good for you, cut it out otherwise it will become like cancer and can destroy you. Our thoughts based on the five sensory systems which are the precursors to our emotions and the actions we take. Mastering our minds will help us to manage the thoughts that plays in our minds, affecting how we feel, what we do, and what comes out of our mouths.

We should never ignore our "gut feeling." Many times before we feed our thought, we have a "gut feeling" that we ignore. If you don't feel good about something, don't pursue it. Sometimes it could be something simple like going over to visit a friend. You are aware your friend is into things you have been working on in your personal life (drinking alcohol, using street drugs, pornography, video games, and so on). You are aware every time you visit your friend, you end up doing things you should not do. If you have a "gut feeling", ignore it and put a peace to the warning thoughts by exploring all the things that can go wrong. Be alert and aware. Many of us usually gets trapped into deciding against our "gut feeling," and have regrets.

Some of the choices we make triggers our past creating more psychological issues affecting our mental health. When we develop unhealthy coping strategies, they can become our default mode to cope when under stress. The mind will lead you to fall into old habits. However when we master our mind, we can chose alternatives that are new which we can set as new default modes. The healthy neuropathways. An example would be someone who used to use alcohol to cope. The individual may choose to drink club soda with a lime or lemon to avoid drinking alcohol especially at family events. It is a parallelism to the old pathway. Some individuals may choose to set themselves to have one drink which is monitored by their spouse or family member as a healthy way to drink alcohol, which is another parallelism. Street drugs, misuse of prescription medications, gambling, and other addictions are considered unhealthy copying strategies which need new healthy parallelism to cope with life's stressors.

Another interesting thought is learning to say 'No.' The desire to say "no" when we have all intentions to say "yes". If we yield ourselves to what is being asked that is not in our favour, it may lead us to fall into a trap that stimulates negative thoughts. Learning to say "no" is okay and that is one thought we should have flowing in our minds. Some people say yes all the time working all types of extra shifts, helping others move, going to different functions when asked, making donations to everyone who asks, buying items when on sale, buying from door-to-door sellers, going to their friend's sports games, and so on. Learning to say no will help to stay focused on what is most important. Learning to prioritize what is most important will help to become more progressive in life. And this will be another perfect example of mastering the mind, when not driven by impulsivity.

We need to control our assumptions as they can condition the mind to carry the wrong message. Controlling our thoughts from the assumption of what is being texted, emailed, or on the phone. So many time we make a presumption as to what we read, not knowing the full story or the content of what is being written. Some people may have difficulty expressing themselves over the phone, in texting, and emailing. Developing a thought which is usually negative about a phone call, a text, or an email will play in your mind like a movie. The best is face-to-face or making sure you understand the person you are communicating with before you allow your thought to create a conclusion. It's easy to create thoughts, but they can be very challenging to get rid of.

We need to control planting negative thoughts since they are like weeds that can take over our mind from the fruitfulness of being or staying positive. How many of us try to convince others to like what we like, or steer a conversation for others to adapt or engage in? We then become frustrated when the conversation is not going the way we assumed in our minds. We try to make our only conclusion about what the other person's reaction is, what they may say, their mood, how they dress, and their non-verbal language. We try to control others by how we carry on a conversation and not monitoring that we are the dominant ones in the conversation. We speak words to stir the person's emotion or awaken their thoughts, especially if we know some of their weakness or what they have an interest in. We try to live like sales' people, sharing our thoughts to get others to share and then plant our thought seeds into their minds.

Some of us hide our insecurity by speaking negatively about everyone. We have nothing good to say and allow our thoughts that are being created to be negative. Everyone we speak with, we speak to them about someone else. We only see negative attributes and nothing positive comes out of our month. We may not see it and the people we associate with it would not say anything since they want to hear the gossip. Although they are aware that the person who is speaking negatively is also speaking negatively about them behind their back, they continue to feed the person's ego. Negativity feeds on your life and will draw joy from your heart. It's better to walk away and refocus your thoughts on something healthy for the mind.

We have the ability to be resilient. Which means we can train our minds to stay positive, even as we develop our dreams, set goals for our lives, work on plans, and stay on track. We are in control of our thoughts and can do whatever we put our mind to do. We have more control over our thoughts than we may give ourselves credit for. We need to utilize the power of our thought to change the world around us.

With that being said, we need to manage our impulsivity in making decisions, responding to conversations, buying things and voicing our opinions especially when we were not asked to share it. Some of us can be impulsive and have an automatic reaction when others speak to us. It's like if someone were to attempt to hit us, we block ourselves from being hurt. We have a automatic reaction in which at times we can say things that can be offensive toward others and bring emotional harm to ourselves. We need to learn how to manage these automatic thoughts and allow our emotional skills to be a thicker than tomato skin. We all need to consider how we should respond to others if they enforce their thoughts on us. What would be your reaction and how would you psychologically deal with it? Some of us can be defensive with what we say, harsh, cold, emotionless, and unrealistic. We need to consider what we give out, others will react the same and lash back. We all need to learn to be realistic in how we behave with what we say. We should ask ourselves " is it logical," "are we watching the tone of our voices," "are we being "black and white" in our conversation, not willing to listen to those who are in the grey?" "Are we being mindful that others may have value in what they are saying as much as what we say?"

We need to learn how to be our defense lawyer and cross-exam ourselves to ensure that we are accommodating others as much as we want others to accommodate us. Learning the process of how we think and what we may need to change to associate with others is important, otherwise, we may live with a delusion that others want to be in our presence when in reality they are afraid of telling us the truth of how they feel about us. We need to learn to recognize our limitations and speak to others with an understanding that we can make mistakes and is opened for corrections. We need to acknowledge that others have tons of value to add to the conversation. We will carry a long conversation without making others feel they are walking on eggshells. This is a good sign that we are mastering our minds and taking control of our thoughts.

We need to learn that some things we think, we need to put on the shelf, especially if becomes an obstacle in our relationships with others. Learning that our mind can think faster than we can comprehend and the need not to act on what we think at times is healthy. Mastering the mind gives us that power to be in control, especially when we can remind ourselves that we don't have to give an answer to every question, we don't have to react to every emotion from others, we don't have to be impulsive, and that time is our best friend. We can always give an answer when the dust settles, and we give ourselves some time to process a conversation that may be tense. Mastering the mind is being able to weed out anything that may come across harmful, demanding, questioning, parenting and objective.

THE *Three* MINDS

The power of the human mind is a vast and complex phenomenon that has captivated philosophers, psychologists, and scientists for centuries. It is within the realms of our minds that our thoughts, emotions, and decision-making processes converge, shaping our perceptions of the world and influencing the course of our lives. We need to understand the intricate interplay between the emotional mind, reasonable mind, and wise mind. We need to unravel the distinct aspects of each mind and explore how they contribute to our understanding of ourselves and the world around us.

Negotiating with our own minds can often be a challenging endeavour. Our thoughts, emotions, and desires may sometimes pull us in different directions, creating inner conflicts and dilemmas. There is an art of negotiation within our own minds, seeking to find common ground, identify our true values and motivations, and forge a harmonious alliance between the emotional, reasonable, and wise minds.

THE THREE MINDS

At the core of our mental landscape lies the emotional mind, which serves as a wellspring of feelings, passions, and impulses. Our emotional minds play a significant role in our daily lives, influencing our perceptions, feelings, opinions, actions, and the decisions we make. It can shape our decision-making processes, clouding our judgment or leading us astray, while at other times offering valuable insights and guiding us towards optimal outcomes. Our emotional minds can be viewed as a tomato; it has thin skin and can feel everything including verbal and nonverbal communications from others. This can create issues as we react to how we feel and not considering the logics and facts behind the thought or action taken in making a decision or adding resolutions. Tomatoes are usually juicy and sweet but can be damage very easily.

Our emotional minds are contagious, and the emotions of others can influence our decision making. When we are surrounded by individuals expressing strong emotions, it can affect our own emotional state and consequently impact our choices. For instance, in a group setting, if there is a prevalent sense of enthusiasm for a particular option, we may be more inclined to follow the crowd and make decisions based on the collective emotional atmosphere. It is crucial to recognize this influence and assess whether our decisions align with our individual values and goals.

Our emotion minds can introduce biases into decision making, leading us to favour certain options or perspectives based on our emotional state. For example, if we are feeling anxious or fearful, we may be more likely to choose the safest or most familiar option, even if it is not the most optimal. On the other hand, positive emotions can lead to overconfidence and risk-taking. Being aware of these biases can help us critically evaluate our decisions and consider alternative perspectives.

The emotional minds can be wounded for years if not cared for and not considering the bigger picture in life. If we focus on the negative feeling that comes from its wounds, we will not allow ourselves to be healed. When the emotional mind rules, it is easy for us to react impulsively without thinking of what is being said at the moment. Our primary thought is spoken and not our secondary thought which is our processed thoughts.

Our emotional minds regulation refers to the ability to manage and control our emotions effectively. Making decisions under the influence of intense emotions, such as anger or sadness, can cloud our judgment and lead to impulsive or irrational choices. Developing emotional intelligence and self-awareness allows us to recognize and regulate our emotions, creating a space for more reasoned decision making. It is easy to feel everyone is against us because they did not agree with us. When people agree with us, we see them as friends but that can change from zero to a hundred the moment they disagree. Learning to agree to disagree can be problematic as we have difficult understanding that concept. We need to understand our emotions can be negative but can also be positive. Learning to grow the positive emotional mind can be a struggle, but not impossible.

When faced with a decision, our emotional mind can strongly influence our thought processes and subsequent actions. Our emotions such as fear, anger, or excitement can cloud our judgment and lead us to make impulsive or irrational choices. On the other hand, emotions can also provide valuable insights and intuitive signals about our preferences, values, and desires. It is important to acknowledge and understand our emotions without letting them overpower our reasoning abilities.

The emotional mind can be viewed as part of our consciousness that is driven by emotions, feelings, and desires. It is responsible for our immediate and instinctual reactions to various stimuli. This is one reason why when we live with developing the emotional mind as the dominant mind, we can be hurt easily by what we don't want to hear. We can be easily suicidal or harm ourselves very frequently. We can become sexually active with multiple partners, have difficult making decisions and sees the world as our enemy. We may find it a challenge to take constructive criticism and maintain a stable job as we don't like being told what to do.

The emotional mind is highly influential in decision making as it can colour our perceptions, bias our judgments, and drive impulsive actions. When operating solely from the emotional mind, we may find ourselves making decisions based on temporary emotional states rather than careful consideration. It is essential to understand how our emotional minds can both enhance and hinder our decision-making abilities.

Our emotional minds can serve as intuitive signals, providing us with valuable information about a situation or person. Our gut feelings and instincts often arise from subconscious processing, integrating past experiences and stored knowledge. While it is important to trust our intuition, it is equally important to balance it with rational analysis. By acknowledging and exploring our intuitive signals, we can gain deeper insights into our decision-making processes.

While our emotional minds can introduce biases, they can also provide valuable insights into our preferences, values, and desires. Engaging with our emotions allows us to connect with our authentic selves and make decisions that align with our true needs and aspirations. By acknowledging and understanding our emotions, we can integrate them into the decision-making process, using them as a guide rather than letting them dominate our choices.

Recognizing the influence of emotions on decision making is a crucial step towards achieving a balance between the emotional mind and the reasonable mind. By cultivating self-awareness, emotional intelligence, and the ability to regulate our emotions, we can make more informed and balanced decisions. Incorporating both reason and emotions in the decision-making process enables us to tap into the wisdom of the wise mind, leading to outcomes that align with our values and promote overall well-being.

While our emotional minds provide a crucial input, it is essential to recognize the role of logic and rationality in sound decision making. The reasonable mind represents the realm of logical thinking, facts, rationalization, objective analysis, and critical reasoning. This mind can help us evaluate information, weigh the pros and cons, and make informed choices, thereby offering a counterbalance to the sometimes overwhelming influence of emotions.

Balancing our emotional and reasonable minds are crucial for making optimal decisions and achieving favourable outcomes. Both the emotional and reasonable mind play significant roles in our decision-making processes, and finding the right balance between them is essential for making well-informed and thoughtful choices.

The reasonable mind is essential for critical thinking, problem-solving, and weighing the pros and cons of different options. However, when the reasonable mind dominates decision making, it can lead to a lack of empathy or disregard for the emotional impact of choices. This mind are more dominant in most men as they find it difficult to be emotional, especially when emotions was viewed as a sense of weakness.

The reasonable mind can be viewed as a cantaloupe, sweet inside but has a thick skin outside. When this mind dominated a person, they can have difficult relating and connecting to others. They can have insecurities and lack of confidence in themselves, so not sharing their emotions makes them feel safe.

However, achieving optimal outcomes often lies in finding a delicate balance between the emotional and reasonable minds. The ability to integrate and harmonize these two aspects can lead to more nuanced and effective decision making. We need to balance our emotions with rationality, allowing for a more comprehensive understanding of complex situations and fostering the development of optimal solutions.

The reasonable mind play a crucial role in sound decision making. While our emotional minds provide valuable insights and inform our preferences, it is essential to balance them with logical reasoning to make informed choices. By engaging the reasonable mind, we can evaluate situations objectively, consider relevant facts and evidence, and assess the potential outcomes of our decisions.

The reasonable mind guide us in collecting and analysing relevant information before making a decision. We can use critical thinking skills to assess the credibility and reliability of the sources, identify biases, and weigh the evidence. By relying on objective data and facts, we can make decisions based on a solid foundation.

Applying the reasonable mind helps us identify cause and effect relationships within a decision-making context. By understanding the potential consequences of different choices, we can evaluate the long-term implications and consider the ripple effects that each option may have. This analysis allows us to make choices that align with our goals and values.

The reasonable mind enable us to assess the probability and risk associated with different outcomes. By examining the available information, we can estimate the likelihood of various scenarios and consider the potential benefits and drawbacks of each. This evaluation allows us to make more calculated decisions, weighing the potential rewards against the associated risks.

Cognitive biases are inherent tendencies that can lead to irrational decision making. By engaging the reasonable mind, we can recognize and mitigate these biases. Logical reasoning helps us identify when our thinking might be influenced by cognitive biases such as confirmation bias (favouring information that confirms pre-existing beliefs) or anchoring bias (relying too heavily on initial information). By consciously challenging these biases, we can make more objective decisions.

Deductive reasoning involves drawing specific conclusions from general principles, while inductive reasoning involves forming general principles based on specific observations. Both forms of reasoning can be valuable in decision making. Deductive reasoning allows us to apply existing knowledge and rules to reach logical conclusions, while inductive reasoning allows us to form hypotheses and generate new insights. By employing these forms of reasoning, we can think systematically and consider multiple perspectives.

The reasonable mind helps us weigh the pros and cons of different options. By objectively evaluating the advantages and disadvantages of each alternative, we can identify the potential benefits and drawbacks associated with them. This process enables us to make more informed decisions that align with our goals and values.

The reasonable mind encourages us to consider the long-term implications of our decisions. It helps us think beyond immediate gratification or short-term gains and consider the impact of our choices on our future well-being. By aligning our decisions with our long-term goals, we can make choices that promote our overall growth and fulfilment.

Engaging in the reasonable mind involves seeking input and feedback from others. By considering different perspectives and inviting diverse opinions, we can enhance the quality of our decision making. Rationality allows us to objectively evaluate the input received, weigh its relevance, and integrate it into our decision-making process.

By recognizing the importance of the reasonable mind and bringing a balance with the emotional mind, we can leverage these cognitive tools to make more sound and informed decisions. Embracing the reasonable mind alongside the emotional and wise minds allows us to achieve a balanced approach, considering both the facts and our emotional responses. Ultimately, this integration leads to decisions that are not only well-reasoned but also aligned with our values, emotions, and long-term goals.

To strike a balance between our emotional and reasonable minds, it is essential to develop self-awareness and introspection. Being aware of our emotional state and its potential impact on decision making allows us to take a step back and assess the situation more objectively. Mindfulness practices can be immensely helpful in cultivating this self-awareness and reducing impulsive reactions driven solely by emotions.

An effective strategy for balancing our emotional and reasonable minds is to acknowledge and validate our emotions while also subjecting them to critical scrutiny. This involves acknowledging and understanding the emotions we experience, recognizing their influence on our thoughts and actions, and then critically evaluating whether these emotions align with the logical aspects of the decision at hand.

In some cases, our emotional and reasonable minds may appear to be in conflict, pulling us in different directions. In such situations, it can be helpful to seek additional information, advice, or perspectives from trusted individuals. Engaging in open and honest discussions with others can provide valuable insights and help us gain a broader understanding of the situation, enabling us to find a more harmonious balance between emotions and reason.

Ultimately, achieving a balance between our emotional and reasonable minds requires practice and conscious effort. It involves recognizing the strengths and limitations of both aspects and finding ways to integrate them effectively. By acknowledging our emotions, harnessing the power of reason, and subjecting our decisions to thoughtful analysis, we can make more well-rounded choices that align with our values, goals, and overall well-being.

Remember that finding the right balance between emotions and reason is a dynamic process, and it may vary depending on the context and nature of the decision. With time and practice, you can develop the ability to navigate the complexities of decision making, tapping into both the emotional and rational aspects of your mind to achieve optimal outcomes.

The wise mind encompasses a harmonious integration of both the emotional and reasonable minds. It is a state of balanced decision making that combines the wisdom of emotions with the clarity of rationality. The wise mind involves accessing our intuition, inner wisdom, and deeper understanding of ourselves and the situation at hand. When we tap into the wise mind, we make decisions that align with our values, consider the emotions of ourselves and others, and take into account the long-term consequences.

Beyond the emotional and reasonable minds lies the concept of the wise mind, which represents the synthesis of intuition, insight, and deep understanding. The wise mind draws upon the wisdom of our experiences, the integration of our emotional and rational faculties, and a profound sense of self-awareness. We will explore how cultivating the wise mind can enhance our decision-making capabilities and lead to outcomes that are aligned with our values, aspirations, and long-term well-being.

Understanding these different aspects of the mind is crucial because it allows us to recognize the strengths and limitations of each. By becoming aware of how our emotions and reasoning influence our decision making, we can cultivate a greater sense of self-awareness and make more informed choices.

The wise mind play a significant role in decision making, complementing the rational and logical aspects of the mind. While our emotional and reasonable minds have their place, intuition offers a unique perspective that can lead to innovative solutions and successful outcomes. This can be considered the wise mind. When our emotional and reasonable minds are combined and balanced together, we can grow the wise mind.

Integrating the wise mind into decision-making processes involves

THE THREE MINDS

tapping into your subconscious knowledge and relying on your instincts. We can then harness what is best for us, others and integrate effective decision making for the future.

The wise mind can be described as a deep, instinctual understanding that arises without conscious reasoning. It involves accessing information and patterns that may not be immediately evident to the conscious mind. Intuitive insights often manifest as sudden "aha" moments, strong feelings, or a sense of certainty. While intuition is difficult to define and quantify, it is a valuable tool that can guide decision-making processes.

The wise mind are visceral responses that emerge from our core being. They can be described as a "knowing" or a strong sensation that something is right or wrong. These feelings are often tied to our body's physiological responses, such as a quickening heartbeat or a tightening sensation in the stomach. Trusting our gut feelings means paying attention to these bodily sensations and acknowledging them as valuable inputs in the decision-making process.

The wise mind should not be seen as a replacement for rationality and logic but rather as a complement to them. Striking a balance between intuition and rationality involves considering both aspects when making decisions. While rationality provides a systematic and analytical approach, the wise mind can offer a broader perspective that takes into account subtle cues and subconscious knowledge. By integrating the two, we can arrive at more holistic and well-informed decisions.

Developing the wise mind requires cultivating self-awareness and practicing mindfulness. By becoming more attuned to our thoughts, feelings, and bodily sensations, we can gain insights into our intuitive processes. Regular meditation and mindfulness exercises can help us quiet the noise of the conscious mind and tap into our wise mind. Additionally, paying attention to past experiences and reflecting on instances when our wise mind proved accurate, can help build trust in our intuitive abilities.

While the wise mind can be a powerful tool, it is important to validate and test our insights when making important decisions. This can involve gathering additional information, seeking diverse perspectives, or conducting experiments to confirm or refute our intuitive hunches. By combining intuitive insights with evidence-based reasoning, we can make more robust decisions and minimize the risk of being swayed solely by emotions or biases.

The wise mind often thrives in situations that require creative problem-solving and innovation. By embracing the wise mind, we open ourselves up to novel ideas, alternative perspectives, and unconventional solutions. This can be particularly valuable in complex and ambiguous situations where relying solely on rationality may not lead to optimal outcomes. The wise mind can help us think outside the box and consider possibilities that may have been overlooked by a purely analytical approach.

Developing the wise mind is a crucial aspect of harnessing the power of our minds. It enables us to adapt to changing circumstances, navigate complex challenges, and generate innovative solutions. The wise mind includes embracing diverse perspectives, questioning assumptions, and embracing uncertainty, as we strive for better problem-solving abilities.

Developing the wise mind is a crucial skill for better problem-solving, as it allows individuals to adapt their thinking and approach to different situations. Understanding the concept of the wise mind is the first step towards developing this skill. It involves the ability to shift between different the emotional and reasonable mind, such as feelings, attention, perception, facts, logics and rationalizations and problem-solving strategies, in response to changing circumstances.

To enhance the wise mind it is important to adopt a growth mindset. Believing that your abilities and intelligence can be developed through effort and learning allows you to approach problems with a more open and flexible mindset. Embracing a growth mindset encourages you to seek out challenges and view setbacks as opportunities for growth, which in turn enhances your ability to adapt and find creative solutions.

Another effective way to enhance the wise mind is by embracing novel experiences. Engaging in activities that expose you to new information, ideas, and perspectives can broaden your thinking and stimulate cognitive flexibility. This can involve reading diverse books, exploring different cultures, learning new skills, or engaging in creative hobbies. By exposing yourself to a variety of experiences, you expand your mental repertoire and become more adaptable in your thinking.

Practicing perspective-taking is another valuable strategy for the development of the wise mind. By actively putting yourself in someone else's shoes and considering alternative viewpoints, you develop a greater understanding of different perspectives and increase your capacity to consider a wider range of solutions to problems. This exercise allows you to break free from rigid thinking patterns and encourages you to explore new possibilities.

Engaging in intellectually challenging activities is also beneficial for developing the wise mind. Puzzles, brainteasers, strategy games, and other mentally stimulating tasks require you to think critically, analyse situations from different angles, and adapt your approach based on new information. These activities train your brain to be more flexible and adaptable in problem-solving situations.

Being comfortable with uncertainty and ambiguity is another important aspect of the wise mind. Embracing the unknown allows you to explore new possibilities and consider alternative solutions. Recognizing that not all problems have clear-cut answers and that there can be multiple paths to reach a solution frees you from rigid thinking and encourages more innovative problem-solving.

Challenging your assumptions and beliefs is also essential for developing the wise mind. By questioning your own preconceived notions, you open yourself up to new ideas and perspectives. This mindset shift can lead to more creative problem-solving and the discovery of alternative solutions that you may not have considered before.

Practicing divergent thinking is another effective way to grow the wise mind. Divergent thinking involves generating multiple creative solutions to a problem. Engaging in brainstorming exercises or creative activities that encourage you to think beyond conventional boundaries expands the wise mind and encourages you to consider a wide range of possibilities. This approach allows for more innovative problem-solving and helps overcome mental rigidity.

When it comes to decision-making, we often find ourselves in a constant internal negotiation between our emotional mind, reasonable mind, and wise mind. These three aspects of the mind represent different perspectives and influences that shape our choices and actions. Negotiating with your own mind involves finding a harmonious balance between these three aspects to make informed and well-rounded decisions.

To begin the process of negotiating with your own mind, it's important to cultivate self-awareness. This means recognizing and acknowledging your emotional responses, thoughts, and biases that may influence your decision-making. By understanding your own mental states, you can better navigate through conflicting emotions and thoughts that may arise during the decision-making process.

One key aspect of negotiating with your own mind is the ability to differentiate between the emotional and reasonable mind. The emotional mind can provide valuable insights and guide us towards what matters most to us, but they can also cloud our judgment and lead to impulsive decisions. The reasonable mind, on the other hand, emphasizes logic, facts, and objective analysis. By acknowledging the role of both the

THE THREE MINDS

emotional and reasonable minds, we can strive for a balanced approach that takes into account both the heart and the mind.

To negotiate effectively with your own mind, it is crucial to develop emotional intelligence. Emotional intelligence involves recognizing, understanding, and managing your own emotions, as well as empathizing with the emotions of others. By honing your emotional intelligence, you can navigate through difficult emotions, such as fear or anger, and make decisions that are not solely driven by intense emotional reactions.

Furthermore, integrating the wise mind into the decision-making process is essential. While logic and reasoning play a significant role, our wise mind provide valuable insights that go beyond rational analysis. The wise mind is often based on subconscious processing of information and can provide a holistic understanding of a situation. By listening to your wise mind and combining it with rational thinking, you can tap into a deeper level of wisdom and make more holistic decisions.

The wise mind is crucial for negotiating with your own minds. This gives you the ability to adapt your thinking, perspectives, and strategies when faced with new information or changing circumstances. By being open-minded and willing to consider alternative viewpoints, you can challenge your own preconceptions and expand your range of possibilities. The wise mind helps you avoid getting stuck in rigid thinking patterns and enables you to explore creative solutions to problems.

Remember, integrating the wise mind into decision making is not about dismissing rationality or emotions, but about harnessing the collective power of the emotional mind, reasonable mind, and wise mind. By acknowledging and embracing all these aspects of our minds, we can achieve a harmonious and balanced approach to decision making, leading to more satisfying and successful outcomes.

Developing the ability to navigate between the emotional,

reasonable, and wise minds is a skill that can be honed through practice. It requires cultivating emotional intelligence, enhancing cognitive flexibility, and nurturing mindfulness. The ultimate goal is to find harmony and balance within these aspects of the mind, allowing us to make decisions that are both emotionally satisfying and logically sound.

In conclusion, exploring the power of the mind and understanding its different aspects can greatly enhance our decision-making abilities and overall well-being. Throughout this chapter, we have delved into the intricate workings of the emotional mind, the reasonable mind, and the wise mind. By unravelling these distinct facets, we have gained valuable insights into how our thoughts, emotions, and reasoning processes influence our choices and actions.

Negotiating with our own minds is an art that requires patience, self-compassion, and practice. Recognizing when our emotional mind or our reasonable mind dominates our decision-making process empowers us to consciously shift our focus and tap into the wisdom of the wise mind. It is through this negotiation that we find alignment and synergy within ourselves, facilitating more harmonious and balanced decision-making.

Understanding the power of the mind involves unravelling its various aspects and embracing the interplay between the emotional mind, reasonable mind, and wise mind. By recognizing the influence of our emotions, incorporating logical thinking, integrating intuition, cultivating cognitive flexibility, and negotiating with ourselves, we can achieve harmony and balance within our decision-making process. With this awareness and skill set, we are better equipped to navigate the complexities of life, make choices that align with our values, and ultimately foster personal growth and well-being.

DEVELOP *Mental* TOUGHNESS

Developing Mental Toughness explores a wide range of strategies and techniques that can help you cultivate and strengthen your mental resilience. By embracing these practices, you will be well-equipped to navigate the challenges and obstacles that life presents with a positive mindset and unwavering determination.

Mental toughness is not an innate quality reserved for a select few; rather, it is a skill that can be developed and honed over time. It enables you to face adversity head-on, bounce back from setbacks, and flourish in the face of change. By focusing on the power of your mind, you can unlock the potential within you to overcome obstacles and thrive in all areas of your life.

To have a better understanding of mental toughness we need to explore the mental fortitude that will empower us to thrive in any

DEVELOP MENTAL TOUGHNESS

situation. It will equip us with the tools and knowledge needed to cultivate a positive and resilient mindset, enabling us to face challenges head-on and persevere even when the going gets tough.

Remember, developing mental toughness is a continuous process. It requires dedication, practice, and a commitment to personal growth. As we embark mental toughness, be open to new perspectives and willing to embrace change. With each step you take, you will discover the remarkable strength within you, empowering you to conquer obstacles, achieve your goals, and live a fulfilling life.

One of the key foundations to mental toughness lies in recognizing and challenging negative self-talk. Our minds have an incredible power to shape our reality, and the way we talk to ourselves internally can greatly influence our emotions, behaviours, and overall well-being. We can rewire our brains to transform negative self-talk into positive and empowering affirmations.

Negative self-talk often manifests as self-criticism, doubt, and limiting beliefs that hold us back from reaching our full potential. It acts as a roadblock to our growth and can significantly impact our confidence and self-esteem. However, by consciously recognizing these negative thought patterns, we can begin the process of rewiring our brain for positive change.

By becoming aware of our negative self-talk, we gain the power to challenge and replace these destructive thoughts with more positive and supportive ones. This process involves reframing our perspective and cultivating self-compassion. Instead of berating ourselves for perceived shortcomings or failures, we can choose to respond with kindness and understanding.

Change is an inevitable part of life, and developing mental toughness involves embracing it with a positive and open mindset. We need to tap into the transformative power of embracing change and cultivating adaptability, and how these qualities can contribute to your overall mental toughness.

Change provides us with opportunities for growth, self-discovery, and personal development. By embracing change, we open ourselves up to new possibilities, experiences, and perspectives. Rather than fearing or resisting change, we can choose to see it as a catalyst for progress and transformation.

One of the key aspects of developing mental toughness is recognizing that change is often accompanied by uncertainty and the unknown. It requires a willingness to step outside of our comfort zone and explore uncharted territories. By doing so, we broaden our horizons and expand our capabilities, fostering personal growth and resilience.

Adaptability goes hand in hand with embracing change. It is the ability to adjust and thrive in different situations, even when circumstances are constantly evolving. A mentally tough individual possesses the flexibility and resilience to adapt their mindset, strategies, and actions to meet the demands of a changing environment.

When we cultivate adaptability, we develop a remarkable ability to navigate challenges and setbacks effectively. Instead of becoming overwhelmed or discouraged by unexpected circumstances, we see them as opportunities to learn, evolve, and find creative solutions. This mindset allows us to maintain a sense of control and optimism, even when faced with adversity.

Moreover, embracing change and cultivating adaptability can lead to increased self-confidence and self-belief. As we navigate new experiences and overcome obstacles, we develop a deep-rooted trust in our ability to handle whatever comes our way. This self-assurance becomes a solid foundation for our mental toughness, enabling us to face future challenges with unwavering resolve.

In the realm of mental toughness, few attributes are as transformative as a growth mindset. A growth mindset is a powerful belief that our abilities and intelligence can be developed and improved through dedication, effort, and a willingness to learn. It is the belief that challenges are opportunities for growth, and setbacks are merely stepping stones on the path to success. By cultivating a growth mindset, we open ourselves up to a world of possibilities and unleash our true potential.

Embracing a growth mindset is an invitation to view failures not as permanent limitations, but as valuable lessons and opportunities for growth. Instead of being discouraged by setbacks, those with a growth mindset approach them with curiosity and resilience. They see obstacles as puzzles to solve and setbacks as temporary roadblocks on the journey toward their goals. They see obstacles as opportunities and failures as fertilizers for their future.

One of the most remarkable aspects of a growth mindset is its ability to reshape the way we perceive our own abilities and potential. With a growth mindset, we understand that intelligence and talents are not fixed traits but rather qualities that can be developed over time. This realization liberates us from the constraints of self-imposed limitations and allows us to embrace continuous learning and improvement.

By cultivating a growth mindset, we become more open to taking on challenges outside of our comfort zone. We must recognize that stepping into the unknown is an opportunity for personal and professional growth. This willingness to push boundaries and embrace new experiences fosters resilience and adaptability, crucial qualities for navigating the ever-changing landscape of life.

Moreover, a growth mindset encourages a positive attitude towards effort and perseverance. Instead of viewing hard work as a burden, individuals with a growth mindset see it as an essential component of growth and success. They understand that with consistent effort and deliberate practice, they can achieve mastery in any area of their choosing.

Furthermore, a growth mindset nurtures a love for learning. It encourages a thirst for knowledge, the exploration of new ideas, and a willingness to seek out feedback and constructive criticism. This continuous pursuit of learning fuels personal and professional growth, propelling individuals towards their goals with an unwavering determination.

Cultivating a growth mindset can be developed and strengthened over time. Practice self-compassion and embrace a positive and patient attitude towards your own growth. Celebrate your progress and the small victories along the way, for they are stepping stones towards your larger aspirations.

Setting realistic goals is a vital component of developing mental toughness. It involves envisioning our desired outcomes and creating a roadmap to achieve them. By setting clear, achievable goals, we lay the foundation for success and create a positive mindset that propels us forward.

When setting our goals, it's crucial to strike a balance between ambition and realism. While it's important to challenge ourselves, setting overly ambitious goals can lead to frustration and demotivation if they are consistently out of reach. By setting realistic goals, we create a sense of achievement and momentum, fuelling our motivation and fostering a positive outlook.

In achieving our goals, we will inevitably encounter obstacles along the way. These obstacles may come in various forms, such as unexpected setbacks, self-doubt, or external challenges. However, by cultivating mental toughness, we can overcome these obstacles and continue moving forward towards your aspirations.

Remember, the path to success is rarely a straight line. There will be detours, setbacks, and unexpected hurdles. However, with a positive mindset, realistic goals, and the mental toughness to overcome obstacles, we have the power to navigate these challenges and emerge stronger than ever.

Perseverance, the unwavering determination to keep going despite challenges and setbacks, is a remarkable quality that can propel us towards success and personal growth. There is tremendous power that perseverance holds and how it can contribute to the development of mental toughness in the most positive and uplifting way.

One of the key aspects of developing mental toughness through perseverance is the ability to maintain a positive attitude in the face of adversity. Challenges may seem daunting at first, but by cultivating a mindset focused on finding solutions and learning from setbacks, we can maintain an optimistic outlook even in the toughest of times. With each challenge overcome, our confidence grows, and we become better equipped to face future hurdles.

In today's fast-paced world, stress and anxiety have become increasingly prevalent. However, within the realm of developing mental toughness, we view these challenges as opportunities for growth and self-improvement. We can manage stress and anxiety effectively, empowering ourselves to navigate through life's pressures with grace and resilience.

It is important to recognize that stress and anxiety are natural responses to the demands and uncertainties of everyday life. They are signals from our bodies and minds, indicating the need for attention and care. By adopting a positive perspective, we can transform these experiences into catalysts for personal growth, developing the mental toughness needed to thrive in any situation.

Nurturing our physical, emotional, and mental well-being is crucial for developing mental toughness. Engaging in activities that brings us joy, practicing mindfulness, and prioritizing restful sleep are all integral parts of a self-care routine that can fortify our resilience.

Confidence and self-efficacy are powerful attributes that contribute to mental toughness. When we possess a strong sense of confidence, we believe in our abilities and have faith in our capacity to succeed. Self-efficacy, on the other hand, is the belief in our capability to accomplish specific tasks or goals. Together, they form a dynamic duo that empowers us to overcome challenges and seize opportunities with a positive outlook.

We must practice self-care and engage in activities that nourish our minds, bodies, and spirits. Taking care of ourselves physically and emotionally contributes to a positive self-image and an enhanced sense of self-worth. Engage in activities that brings us happiness, practice self-compassion, and embrace self-acceptance. The more we prioritize self-care, the more our confidence and self-efficacy will flourish.

Building confidence and self-efficacy is an ongoing journey, and it requires patience and perseverance. As we incorporate these strategies into our lives, we will witness a remarkable transformation in how we perceive ourselves and our abilities. With a solid foundation of confidence and self-efficacy, we will approach challenges with resilience, embrace new opportunities, and ultimately achieve our goals with unwavering determination.

In today's fast-paced and increasingly distracted world, the ability to focus and concentrate has become a precious skill. Fortunately, it is a skill that can be cultivated and enhanced through dedicated practice and a positive mindset. There are strategies and techniques that can help us sharpen our focus and concentration, enabling us to achieve greater productivity and success.

When we enhance our focus and concentration, we unlock a world of possibilities. Imagine being able to fully immerse ourselves in a task, free from distractions and interruptions. By developing this skill, we can tap into a state of flow where time seems to slip away, and our productivity soars. Whether we are studying for an important exam, working on a challenging project, or engaging in any activity that requires our undivided attention, the ability to concentrate deeply is a game-changer.

One powerful method to enhance focus and concentration is to create an optimal environment. Designate a specific workspace that is free from clutter and distractions. Minimize external noise and create a comfortable atmosphere that allows our minds to fully engage with the task at hand. By creating a dedicated space for focused work, we signal to our minds that it is time to concentrate, and we eliminate potential sources of interruption.

Another effective strategy is to manage our time effectively. Break our tasks into smaller, manageable chunks and allocate specific time blocks for focused work. Use techniques such as the Pomodoro Technique, where we work in concentrated bursts of time followed by short breaks. This not only helps maintain our focus but also prevents burnout and mental fatigue. With consistent practice, we will find that our ability to concentrate for extended periods improves, and our productivity skyrockets.

In addition to external factors, cultivating a positive mindset is vital for enhancing focus and concentration. Develop a sense of curiosity and interest in the task at hand. Approach it with enthusiasm and a genuine desire to immerse yourself in the subject matter. By cultivating a positive attitude, we create an internal motivation that fuels our focus and concentration, making the experience more enjoyable and rewarding.

Remember, developing enhanced focus and concentration is a gradual process that requires patience and persistence. Celebrate small victories along the way and acknowledge the progress we make, no matter how small. With each dedicated effort, we are building the foundation for a focused and concentrated mind that will empower us to excel in all areas of our lives. By honing this skill, we are setting ourselves up for success and unlocking our full potential. We must unleash our laser-like focus and achieve remarkable results in all our endeavours.

One powerful and transformative tool at our disposal is the practice of mindfulness and meditation. By incorporating these practices into our daily lives, we can cultivate a positive and resilient mindset, enhance our emotional well-being, and strengthen our ability to face challenges with unwavering resolve.

Mindfulness is the art of being fully present and engaged in the present moment, without judgment or attachment. It involves redirecting our attention away from the distractions of the past or future and instead immersing ourselves in the richness of the present experience. Through mindfulness, we develop an acute awareness of our thoughts, emotions, and physical sensations, enabling us to respond to them consciously rather than being swept away by them.

Meditation, on the other hand, is a specific practice that encompasses various techniques aimed at quieting the mind, cultivating inner peace, and fostering self-awareness. It often involves focusing our attention on a particular object, such as our breath or a mantra, to anchor our thoughts and promote a state of calmness and clarity.

When it comes to mental toughness, mindfulness and meditation offer numerous benefits. Firstly, they help us develop an inner strength and resilience by cultivating a deeper understanding of our thoughts and emotions. Through regular practice, we become more adept at recognizing and managing negative thoughts and self-doubt, allowing us to maintain a positive and focused mindset even in challenging situations.

Furthermore, mindfulness and meditation provide us with valuable tools for managing stress and anxiety effectively. By bringing our attention to the present moment, we can detach ourselves from worries about the past or future, reducing the impact of stressors on our mental well-being. These practices promote relaxation and calmness, enabling us to approach difficult situations with a clear and composed mind.

In addition, mindfulness and meditation enhance our ability to concentrate and maintain focus. In a world filled with distractions, cultivating a disciplined mind becomes crucial for mental toughness. By training ourselves to anchor our attention to the present moment through these practices, we can enhance our concentration, heighten our awareness, and stay resilient even in the face of distractions and obstacles.

Moreover, mindfulness and meditation foster self-compassion and self-acceptance. They invite us to observe our thoughts and emotions with curiosity and kindness, without judgment or criticism. This practice of self-compassion enables us to develop a healthy relationship with ourselves, enhancing our self-esteem and self-efficacy.

Ultimately, practicing mindfulness and meditation for mental toughness is a journey of self-discovery and self-mastery. It empowers us to tap into our inner resilience and wisdom, allowing us to respond to life's challenges with grace and fortitude. By incorporating these practices into our daily lives, we embark on a path of personal growth, developing the mental strength and clarity needed to overcome obstacles and thrive in all areas of our lives.

Dedicate time each day to stillness and self-reflection. Embrace the present moment with an open heart and a curious mind. As we embark on this transformative practice, we will unlock the profound potential within ourselves and discover a newfound resilience that will guide us towards a life of strength, purpose, and fulfilment.

In conclusion, we have explored a variety of strategies and techniques aimed at cultivating a positive and resilient mindset. By embracing these practices, we have equipped ourselves with the tools needed to face adversity, overcome challenges, and thrive in all aspects of life.

We began by recognizing the power of challenging negative self-talk and building resilience through adversity. We discovered the transformative effects of embracing change and cultivating adaptability, along with the crucial role of a growth mindset in fostering mental toughness. Setting realistic goals and overcoming obstacles became a cornerstone of our journey, as did harnessing the power of perseverance.

We also delved into managing stress and anxiety effectively, building confidence and self-efficacy, and enhancing focus and concentration. Each of these aspects contributes to our overall mental toughness and empowers us to navigate life's ups and downs with grace and strength.

We explored the profound impact of practicing mindfulness and meditation. By incorporating these practices into our daily lives, we discovered the ability to cultivate a calm and resilient mindset, manage stress, enhance self-awareness, and develop a compassionate relationship with ourselves.

Remember, developing mental toughness is a continuous process. It requires dedication, practice, and a commitment to personal growth. As we move forward, take the knowledge and insights gained from this chapter and apply them in our daily lives. Let's embrace the challenges that come our way as opportunities for growth and learning. Let's celebrate our progress, no matter how small, and be patient with ourselves during setbacks.

Developing mental toughness is not about achieving perfection or never experiencing difficulties. It's about building the resilience and inner strength needed to overcome obstacles, bounce back from setbacks, and thrive amidst the uncertainties of life. It's about developing a mindset that sees challenges as stepping stones to growth and transformation. It's about rewiring our brain.

Let's carry the wisdom and practices gained. Let's embrace the power of our minds, trust in our abilities, and believe in our capacity to face any challenge that comes our way. With mental toughness, we possess the inner strength to persevere, the resilience to bounce back, and the unwavering determination to achieve our goals and live a fulfilling life. We should have confidence, resilience, and a renewed sense of purpose. We can embrace mental toughness, knowing that we have the strength within us to overcome anything that comes our way.

THE POWER *Of* RESILIENCY

In the journey of life, we often encounter challenges, setbacks, and unexpected twists and turns that can leave us feeling overwhelmed and powerless. Yet, there exists within us an incredible capacity to overcome adversity and emerge stronger than before. This capacity is known as resilience, a remarkable trait that enables individuals to navigate the ups and downs of life with grace and fortitude.

In this chapter, we embark on a compelling exploration of the power of resiliency and its profound impact on our lives. We begin by delving into the very essence of resilience, seeking to define its meaning and understand its significance in our personal and professional spheres. By grasping the true nature of resilience, we can harness its potential to transform our experiences and outlook on life.

To comprehend the inner workings of resilience, we turn to the field of neuroscience behind this remarkable quality. We uncover the fascinating processes of brain adaptation and neuroplasticity that underpin resilience, unveiling the remarkable potential for growth and transformation that resides within each of us.

But resilience isn't merely about bouncing back; it's about bouncing back stronger. We explore the art of overcoming setbacks and transforming adversity into opportunities for personal growth and development. By learning from our experiences and embracing the lessons they offer, we can cultivate a deeper sense of resilience and emerge stronger than ever before. Equipped with this newfound understanding, we can explore various strategies and techniques that can be incorporated into our lives. By building a resilience toolkit, we empower ourselves to face challenges head-on, equipped with the tools necessary to navigate life's complexities and emerge triumphant. And with this comes the notion of failure as a stepping stone to success. We must learn how to reframe our perception of failure and leverage it as a catalyst for growth and innovation.

In a world characterized by constant change and uncertainty, resilience becomes an invaluable asset. We embrace the concept of uncertainty and change, recognizing them as catalysts for personal and collective transformation. By reframing our perspective and embracing the unknown, we can cultivate a resilient mindset that enables us to adapt and thrive in the face of uncertainty.

We must turn our attention to the realm of relationships, recognizing that resilience extends beyond the individual and is equally applicable in our interactions with others. Navigating conflict and adversity within relationships requires a unique set of skills, and we explore how resilience plays a crucial role in fostering healthy connections, enabling us to weather storms and cultivate meaningful relationships that stand the test of time. By understanding and harnessing the power of resilience, we empower ourselves to embrace life's challenges, transform setbacks into opportunities, and cultivate a resilience that allows us to thrive in an ever-changing world.

Resiliency refers to the ability to bounce back, recover, and adapt in the face of adversity, setbacks, or challenging circumstances (Masten, A. S., 2018). It is the capacity to withstand and recover from difficult life events, such as personal or professional failures, loss, trauma, or stress. Resilience is not about avoiding or eliminating challenges but rather about developing the skills and mindset to effectively navigate and overcome them.

Resiliency is a crucial trait to cultivate because life is unpredictable, and everyone experiences hardships at some point. Whether it's a major life crisis or daily stressors, having resilience enables us to cope better, maintain psychological well-being, and thrive in the face of adversity. It acts as a protective factor that helps us maintain mental and emotional equilibrium, enabling us to adapt, learn, and grow from difficult experiences.

When we possess resilience, we are more likely to view setbacks as temporary and solvable challenges, rather than insurmountable obstacles. We display greater perseverance, determination, and a positive mindset, which allows us to remain focused on our goals despite difficulties. Resilient individuals tend to have better problem-solving skills, emotional regulation, and effective coping strategies, which are crucial for managing stress and maintaining mental health.

Resiliency plays a significant role in personal growth and self-development. It allows us to embrace new opportunities, take risks, and step out of our comfort zones. By facing and overcoming challenges, we expand our capabilities, build confidence, and develop a sense of mastery. Resilience fosters a growth mindset, encouraging us to learn from failures, adapt strategies, and continually improve ourselves.

Furthermore, resiliency extends beyond our well-being and has a positive impact on relationships, communities, and society as a whole. Resilient individuals can offer support and encouragement to others during challenging times, contributing to the creation of strong social networks and fostering a sense of collective resilience. They inspire and motivate others by demonstrating that setbacks are not the end, but rather opportunities for growth and transformation.

Resilience is not just a psychological trait; it is also deeply rooted in the science of the brain. Understanding the neural mechanisms behind resilience can shed light on why some of us are better equipped to cope with adversity and bounce back from setbacks.

Neuroplasticity is a key concept in the science of resilience. It refers to the brain's ability to reorganize and rewire itself in response to experiences and environmental changes. The brain is not a fixed and static organ but rather a dynamic and adaptable one. This means that even in the face of adversity, the brain has the potential to change and develop new neural pathways that facilitate resilience.

The brain has the remarkable ability to adapt and recover from traumatic events. One of the key mechanisms underlying neuroplasticity is the formation and strengthening of new neural connections. When faced with adversity, the brain can activate various regions involved in emotional regulation, cognitive processing, and stress response. These regions can then establish new connections and pathways, allowing us to better regulate our emotions, think more clearly, and effectively cope with stress.

The science of resilience is the role of stress hormones, particularly cortisol. In situations of chronic stress, the prolonged release of cortisol can have detrimental effects on the brain, impairing its ability to adapt and respond effectively to challenges. We can regulate our stress response, leading to lower cortisol levels and reduced negative impacts on the brain.

Furthermore, Interactions with supportive and caring individuals can stimulate the release of oxytocin, a hormone that promotes bonding and social connection. Oxytocin has been found to enhance neuroplasticity and increase resilience, as it fosters a sense of safety, trust, and belonging.

Understanding the science of resilience provides valuable insights into how we can cultivate and strengthen our ability to adapt and overcome challenges. It emphasizes the dynamic nature of the brain and its capacity for growth and change. By actively engaging in activities that promote neuroplasticity, including learning new skills, engaging in mindfulness practices, seeking social support, and maintaining a positive mindset, we can enhance our resilience and build a foundation for greater well-being and success in life.

Life is filled with inevitable setbacks and challenges that can often leave us feeling overwhelmed, discouraged, and unsure of how to move forward. However, cultivating resilience enables us to overcome these setbacks and bounce back stronger than before. Resilience is not about avoiding difficulties altogether but rather developing the inner strength and adaptive skills necessary to navigate and recover from adversity.

One key aspect of overcoming setbacks is developing a growth mindset. Instead of viewing setbacks as failures or permanent obstacles, we can see them as opportunities for learning and growth. We must understand that setbacks are a natural part of the learning process and can provide valuable lessons and insights. By reframing setbacks as stepping stones to success, we can approach challenges with a sense of curiosity and resilience.

One aspect of overcoming setbacks is developing effective coping strategies. These strategies may include seeking support from friends, family, or professionals, engaging in self-care activities, or practicing stress-reducing techniques such as mindfulness or meditation. Cultivating a strong support network can provide encouragement, guidance, and a sense of belonging during difficult times.

We must possess strong problem-solving skills. Rather than getting stuck in a cycle of negative thinking or dwelling on the problem, we need to actively seek solutions and take proactive steps towards resolving the issue. This may involve breaking down the problem into smaller, manageable tasks, brainstorming alternative approaches, or seeking advice from others who have faced similar challenges.

Moreover, developing emotional resilience plays a crucial role in overcoming setbacks. We must be emotionally resilient, to recognize and acknowledge our emotions without being overwhelmed by them. We must practice self-compassion and self-acceptance, understanding that it is normal to experience a range of emotions during difficult times. By cultivating emotional resilience, we can bounce back from setbacks more effectively and maintain our overall well-being.

In addition, maintaining a sense of perspective is vital when overcoming setbacks. It is easy to get caught up in the immediate challenges and lose sight of the bigger picture. We must be able to step back and assess the situation from a broader perspective. We need to remind ourselves of our past successes and strengths, which helps maintain optimism and belief in our ability to overcome setbacks.

Resilience involves embracing flexibility and adaptability. Setbacks often require us to adjust our plans, goals, or expectations. We must be open to change and be willing to adapt our strategies or approaches as needed. We can recognize that life is dynamic and unpredictable, and being able to adapt to new circumstances is an essential aspect of resilience.

Developing resiliency is embracing failures as a stepping stone to success. Failure is an inevitable part of life, and our ability to embrace and learn from it is crucial for building resilience and achieving success. Rather than viewing failure as a source of shame or discouragement, we must understand that it is a valuable opportunity for growth, learning, and personal development. By shifting our perspective on failure, we can harness its transformative power and use it as a stepping stone towards future success.

One of the key aspects of embracing failure is reframing it as a learning experience. We must recognize that failure provides valuable feedback and insights that can guide us towards improvement and future success. By approaching failure with curiosity and a willingness to learn, we can extract important lessons and adjust our strategies accordingly. Each failure becomes an opportunity for self-reflection, allowing us to identify areas for growth, refine our skills, and develop new approaches.

Furthermore, embracing failure involves letting go of perfectionism and cultivating a growth mindset. Perfectionism often holds us back from taking risks or trying new things, as we fear the potential for failure. We must understand that perfection is unattainable and that failure is a natural part of the learning process. We embrace a growth mindset, which involves recognizing that abilities and skills can be developed through dedication, effort, and learning from mistakes. By embracing imperfection and nurturing a growth mindset, we free ourselves from the paralyzing fear of failure and open ourselves up to greater opportunities for growth and success.

Embracing failure is developing resilience in the face of setbacks. Failure can be emotionally challenging and may trigger feelings of disappointment, frustration, or self-doubt. We must recognize and acknowledge these emotions without being overwhelmed by them. We can practice self-compassion, treating ourselves with kindness and understanding during difficult times. By cultivating emotional resilience, we can bounce back from failures more effectively, maintaining our motivation and belief in our abilities.

Moreover, viewing failure as a stepping stone to success involves reframing our perception of success itself. We must understand that success is not a linear path, but rather a journey filled with ups and downs. We must recognize that failure is often a necessary part of the process and that setbacks can provide valuable opportunities for growth and redirection. By embracing failure, we develop a more holistic and realistic view of success, one that includes setbacks, challenges, and the perseverance required to overcome them.

Embracing failure requires resilience in the face of external judgment or societal expectations. Society often stigmatizes failure and defines success solely based on achievements and accomplishments. We must challenge these narrow definitions of success and create our own measures of growth and progress. We must recognize that failure is not a reflection of our worth or capabilities but rather an inherent part of the journey towards achieving our goals. By embracing failure and rejecting societal pressures, we free ourselves to pursue our passions, take risks, and reach our full potential.

By reframing failure as a learning experience, letting go of perfectionism, cultivating a growth mindset, developing emotional resilience, redefining success, and rejecting societal expectations, we unlock the transformative power of failure. Through failure, we gain valuable insights, refine our skills, and build the resilience necessary to achieve our goals. Embracing failure allows us to grow, learn, and ultimately thrive on our journey towards success.

Embracing uncertainty and change are constants in life, and our ability to embrace them is essential for building resilience and navigating the ever-evolving world around us. Rather than resisting or fearing uncertainty and change, resilient individuals understand that they are opportunities for growth, learning, and personal development. By embracing uncertainty and change, we can adapt more effectively, discover new possibilities, and thrive in dynamic environments.

Embracing uncertainty involves developing a mindset that is open to the unknown. We must understand that life is unpredictable, and we must approach uncertainty with curiosity and a sense of adventure. We must recognize that uncertainty often brings new opportunities, experiences, and perspectives. By reframing uncertainty as a gateway to growth and exploration, we can cultivate a positive outlook and embrace the possibilities that lie ahead.

Moreover, embracing uncertainty requires flexibility and adaptability. We must be willing to adjust our plans, goals, or expectations in response to changing circumstances. We need to understand that rigid attachment to a particular outcome can hinder progress and resilience. We must embrace a more fluid approach, recognizing that detours and unexpected twists may lead to new and exciting paths. By being open to change and adapting to new situations, we expand our capacity to navigate uncertainty with resilience and creativity.

Embracing change goes hand in hand with embracing uncertainty. We must understand that change is an integral part of growth and progress. We need to recognize that resisting change only leads to stagnation and missed opportunities. We must cultivate a mindset that views change as an essential catalyst for personal and professional development. By embracing change, we open ourselves up to new possibilities, expand our skills and knowledge, and foster a sense of adaptability that strengthens our resilience.

Additionally, embracing uncertainty and change requires developing self-trust and self-confidence. When faced with uncertainty, it is common to experience self-doubt or fear of making the wrong choices. We must trust our abilities and judgment, and have confidence in our capacity to navigate unknown territory. We need to recognize that we have the internal resources to handle whatever comes our way. By cultivating self-trust and self-confidence, we build a solid foundation that enables us to embrace uncertainty and change with resilience and conviction.

Furthermore, embracing uncertainty and change involves cultivating a growth mindset. We must view challenges, setbacks, and new experiences as opportunities for learning and growth. We need to understand that change often brings valuable lessons and insights that contribute to personal development. By maintaining a growth mindset, we approach uncertainty and change with a sense of optimism and a belief that we can adapt, learn, and succeed in new circumstances.

Embracing uncertainty and change requires cultivating patience and self-compassion. Change and uncertainty can be uncomfortable and may trigger feelings of anxiety or vulnerability. We must practice self-compassion, treating ourselves with kindness and understanding during periods of transition. We need to recognize that it is normal to feel uncertain or resistant to change and give ourselves the space and time needed to adjust. By cultivating patience and self-compassion, we navigate uncertainty and change with greater ease, allowing ourselves to grow and thrive in the process.

By adopting a mindset that is open to the unknown, developing flexibility and adaptability, cultivating self-trust and self-confidence, maintaining a growth mindset, and practicing patience and self-compassion, we can navigate uncertainty and change with resilience and embrace the opportunities they bring. Embracing uncertainty and change allows us to expand our horizons, discover new possibilities, and continually evolve on our journey of personal and professional growth.

Resilience plays a crucial role in maintaining healthy and thriving relationships, as conflicts and adversities are inevitable in any interpersonal connection. We must possess the skills and attitudes necessary to navigate these challenges and emerge stronger, fostering deeper connections with others. Building resiliency in relationships involves effective communication, empathy, conflict resolution, and a willingness to learn and grow together.

One key aspect of resiliency in relationships is effective communication. We must prioritize open and honest communication, creating a safe space for sharing thoughts, feelings, and concerns (Bodenmann, G., 2017). We need to actively listen to others without judgment, seeking to understand different perspectives. By fostering clear and respectful communication, we can address conflicts and challenges head-on, preventing issues from escalating and promoting understanding and mutual growth.

We must strive to understand and validate the emotions and experiences of our spouses, partners, friends, and family members. We need to put ourselves in the other person's shoes, practicing active empathy to foster connection and support. By demonstrating empathy, we build trust, strengthen bonds, and create a supportive foundation for navigating adversity together.

Conflict resolution skills are vital for building resiliency in relationships. We must approach conflicts as opportunities for growth and problem-solving rather than as threats to the relationship. We need to engage in constructive dialogue, seeking win-win solutions that address the needs and concerns of all parties involved. We must be open to compromise and be willing to find common ground while maintaining respect and understanding. By skilfully navigating conflicts, we foster resilience in relationships and strengthen our ability to overcome future challenges.

Moreover, resiliency in relationships involves a commitment to learning and personal growth. We must recognize that relationships require ongoing effort and investment. We need to actively seek opportunities for self-reflection, acknowledging our own strengths and areas for improvement. We must be open to feedback and receptive to learning from past mistakes. By embracing a growth mindset and demonstrating a willingness to learn and grow, we foster a culture of resilience within our relationships.

Building resilience in relationships also requires the ability to manage emotions effectively. We must practice emotional regulation, recognizing and managing our own emotions in a healthy and constructive manner. We need to avoid reacting impulsively or engaging in harmful behaviours during times of stress or conflict. By maintaining emotional balance, we create a stable foundation for navigating adversity and maintaining healthy relationships.

Furthermore, resiliency in relationships involves fostering a sense of shared purpose and support. We must recognize the importance of being there for one another during challenging times. We need to provide emotional support, encouragement, and reassurance to our spouses, partners, friends, and family members. By cultivating a sense of shared purpose and offering support, we strengthen our relationships, allowing them to weather storms and bounce back from adversity together.

By practicing effective communication, demonstrating empathy, developing conflict resolution skills, committing to personal growth, managing emotions, and fostering a sense of shared purpose and support, we create strong and thriving connections. Resilience in relationships allows for the mutual growth, understanding, and support needed to overcome challenges, fostering long-lasting and fulfilling relationships.

Building a resilience toolkit is essential for equipping ourselves with a wide range of strategies and techniques to navigate the challenges and uncertainties that life presents. These tools empower us to effectively manage stress, bounce back from setbacks, and maintain our overall well-being. While the specific tools may vary from person to person, there are several fundamental strategies that can contribute to building a robust resilience toolkit.

First and foremost, self-care is a foundational component of resilience. Taking care of our physical, emotional, and mental well-being is crucial for building resilience. This can include practices including regular exercise, proper nutrition, and sufficient sleep to support physical health. Engaging in activities that bring joy, relaxation, and fulfilment helps nurture our emotional well-being. Additionally, practicing mindfulness, meditation, or engaging in hobbies and creative outlets can contribute to maintaining mental well-being. By prioritizing self-care, we build a strong foundation for resilience that enables us to better cope with stress and adversity.

Another vital tool in the resilience toolkit is effective stress management. Chronic stress can take a toll on our well-being and hinder our ability to bounce back from setbacks. Developing healthy coping mechanisms for managing stress is essential. This may involve identifying and engaging in stress-reducing activities that work best for us, such as practicing deep breathing exercises, journaling, engaging in hobbies, or seeking support from trusted individuals. Learning to recognize our stress triggers and developing healthy ways to respond to them empowers us to effectively manage stress and maintain resilience in the face of adversity.

Problem-solving skills are crucial in building resilience. Developing the ability to assess situations, identify potential solutions, and take proactive steps to address challenges strengthens our capacity to overcome setbacks. This involves breaking down problems into manageable parts, brainstorming alternative approaches, and seeking guidance or advice from others when needed. Cultivating a solution-oriented mindset allows us to approach challenges with a sense of empowerment and adaptability, bolstering our resilience in the face of adversity.

Building and maintaining a strong support network is another essential component of a resilience toolkit. Having trusted individuals to lean on during challenging times can provide valuable emotional support, guidance, and perspective. This network can include family, friends, mentors, or support groups. Cultivating meaningful connections and fostering open communication with those around us creates a sense of belonging and reinforces our resilience in times of difficulty. Sharing our experiences, seeking advice, or simply having someone to listen to us can greatly contribute to our ability to bounce back stronger.

Cultivating optimism and practicing positive thinking can be powerful tools in building resilience. Maintaining a positive outlook and reframing challenges as opportunities for growth and learning can help shift our perspective and bolster our ability to overcome setbacks. This does not mean denying the reality of difficult situations, but rather focusing on finding constructive solutions and maintaining a sense of hope and possibility.

Embracing adaptability and flexibility is a vital aspect of a resilience toolkit. Life is often unpredictable, and being able to adjust our plans, goals, and expectations in response to changing circumstances is crucial. When we are resilient we will understand that setbacks and challenges often require adaptation and are willing to embrace change when necessary. This may involve re-evaluating our strategies, considering alternative paths, or being open to new opportunities that may arise.

In conclusion, the power of resiliency is a fundamental aspect of human nature that enables us to navigate the challenges and adversities that life presents. Throughout this chapter, we have explored the multifaceted nature of resilience, from its definition and importance in life to the scientific underpinnings behind its functioning.

Resilience is not a fixed trait but a dynamic quality that can be cultivated and strengthened over time. The science of resilience reveals the remarkable capacity of our brains to adapt and rewire themselves in response to experiences, a phenomenon known as neuroplasticity. This understanding empowers us to embrace setbacks as opportunities for growth and change.

We have delved into various strategies and techniques that can be employed to build our resilience toolkit. From developing strong coping mechanisms to fostering social support networks, these tools equip us with the skills needed to bounce back from adversity and face challenges head-on.

Furthermore, we have discussed the importance of embracing failure as a stepping stone to success. Rather than viewing failure as a roadblock, we can reframe it as a valuable learning experience that fuels personal growth and development.

Embracing uncertainty and change is another vital aspect of resilience. By acknowledging the inevitability of these factors in life, we can adopt a flexible mindset, adapt to new circumstances, and find opportunities for personal and professional advancement.

Lastly, we have explored the role of resiliency in relationships, emphasizing the importance of effective communication, conflict resolution, and navigating adversity together. Building resilient relationships allows us to weather the storms of life, fostering mutual support and growth.

In essence, cultivating resiliency is a lifelong journey that requires dedication, self-reflection, and a willingness to adapt. By integrating the principles and strategies discussed in this chapter into our lives, we can harness the transformative power of resilience and unlock our full potential to overcome challenges, thrive in the face of adversity, and live a more fulfilling and meaningful life.

CHALLENGE *Impulsive* THOUGHTS

We need to embark on a journey of self-reflection and introspection, aiming to understand the nature of impulsive thoughts and uncover the underlying causes that give rise to them. It is important to understand the intriguing realm of impulsive thoughts and explore how they can significantly impact our lives to *"Rewire Your Brain."*

Impulsive thoughts have a way of sneaking into our minds, often leading us to react without much consideration or deliberation. They can manifest in various forms, ranging from spontaneous decisions to sudden bursts of anger or impetuous behaviours. These automatic reactions can have far-reaching consequences, affecting our relationships, mental well-being, and overall quality of life.

To effectively address impulsive thoughts, we first need to recognize and identify them as they arise. By understanding the triggers

CHALLENGE IMPULSIVE THOUGHTS

that prompt these automatic reactions, we can gain greater awareness of our thoughts and emotions in the heat of the moment. Furthermore, understanding our past experiences and how they can shape our impulsive thinking, shedding light on the roots of these patterns and their influence on our present mindset.

Emotions play a significant role in impulsive thoughts. They can act as powerful catalysts, intensifying our automatic reactions and clouding our judgment. By investigating the intricate relationship between emotions and impulsive thinking, we can gain valuable insights into how to navigate and manage these intense feelings more effectively.

Cognitive restructuring lies at the heart of this chapter, offering a powerful tool for reframing our automatic reactions. By subjecting our thoughts to logical examination, we can challenge their validity and consider alternative perspectives. Through the process of cognitive restructuring, we can aim to cultivate a more rational and balanced mindset, enabling us to respond thoughtfully and purposefully to life's challenges.

We need to explore the importance of questioning assumptions and evaluating the validity of our automatic thoughts and beliefs. By actively seeking alternative interpretations and viewpoints, we open ourselves up to a broader range of possibilities, fostering greater flexibility and resilience in our thinking.

Ultimately, our goal should be to equip ourselves with problem-solving strategies rooted in critical thinking. By honing our ability to overcome impulsive thoughts, we can gain the tools needed to navigate life's twists and turns with clarity, wisdom, and emotional well-being.

As we take a transformative journey together as we explore the world of impulsive thoughts, examining and reframing our automatic reactions along the way. We need to *"Rewire Your Brain"* through the landscapes of our minds, as we navigate the path to emotional well-being.

Impulsive thoughts are spontaneous, rapid, and often involuntary mental responses that arise in various situations. These thoughts can be impulsive actions, judgments, or emotional reactions that occur without much forethought or reflection. They tend to arise automatically and can have a significant impact on our lives, influencing our behaviours, decision-making processes, and relationships.

One key characteristic of impulsive thoughts is their immediate nature. They often emerge swiftly, without giving us much time to consider their consequences or evaluate their validity. These thoughts can manifest as impulsive actions, such as making impulsive purchases, engaging in risky behaviours, or saying something without thinking about its potential impact. They can also take the form of impulsive judgments, where we quickly form opinions about others or situations based on limited information or biases.

The impact of impulsive thoughts on our lives can be far-reaching. They can lead to regrettable actions, damaged relationships, and missed opportunities. When we act on impulsive thoughts without considering the potential consequences, we may find ourselves facing unfavourable outcomes or experiencing negative emotions such as guilt, shame, or disappointment.

Impulsive thoughts can also affect our decision-making processes. They often bypass rational thinking and logical analysis, leading us to make hasty or uninformed choices. This can be particularly problematic in situations that require careful consideration, such as financial decisions, career choices, or interpersonal conflicts.

Moreover, impulsive thoughts can influence our relationships with others. When we form quick judgments or react impulsively based on our automatic thoughts, we may misinterpret others' intentions, overlook their perspectives, or engage in conflict unnecessarily. This can lead to misunderstandings, strained relationships, and missed opportunities for empathy and understanding.

CHALLENGE IMPULSIVE THOUGHTS

Understanding the nature and impact of impulsive thoughts is crucial for gaining control over them. By recognizing their spontaneous and automatic nature, we can start to develop strategies to challenge and reframe these thoughts. By exploring the influence of impulsive thoughts on our lives, we can become more aware of their potential drawbacks and seek ways to mitigate their negative impact.

In order to challenge and reframe our impulsive thoughts, it is crucial to first identify them and understand their triggers. Automatic reactions are the thoughts and behaviours that seem to arise automatically and without conscious effort. They often occur in response to certain situations, events, or stimuli, and can have a significant impact on our lives if left unexamined.

Recognizing impulsive thoughts requires a heightened sense of self-awareness. It involves paying close attention to our internal dialogue and emotional responses in different situations. For example, imagine a scenario where you receive constructive criticism from a colleague, a friend or a family member. An impulsive thought in this situation might be something like, "They think I'm incompetent and don't value my work." This automatic reaction might be triggered by feelings of insecurity or a fear of failure.

To identify impulsive thoughts, it is helpful to pause and reflect on our immediate responses to various events. This could involve keeping a journal or making mental notes of situations that elicit strong emotional reactions. By observing our thoughts and emotions without judgment, we can begin to unravel the patterns of our automatic reactions.

It is also important to pay attention to physical cues that accompany impulsive thoughts. These cues can manifest as increased heart rate, tense muscles, or a sudden surge of adrenaline. Being attuned to these bodily sensations can serve as an indicator that impulsive thoughts are arising.

Triggers for impulsive thoughts can vary widely and are unique to each person. They can be linked to past experiences, fears, insecurities, or even certain environments. For instance, someone who has experienced a traumatic event in the past might have impulsive thoughts triggered by situations that resemble or remind them of that event. Triggers can also be more subtle, such as specific words or phrases that evoke strong emotional reactions.

By identifying the triggers associated with our impulsive thoughts, we gain insight into the underlying causes and patterns of our automatic reactions. This awareness allows us to develop strategies to challenge and reframe these thoughts effectively.

Impulsive reactions can often be traced back to underlying causes that influence our thought processes and behaviours. By examining these roots, we gain a deeper understanding of why we react impulsively and can begin to address and manage these reactions more effectively.

One significant factor in impulsive reactions is our individual conditioning and learned behaviours. Throughout our lives, we acquire certain patterns of thinking and acting based on our experiences and the environments we grew up in. If we were raised in a strict and authoritarian household, we might have developed a tendency to react impulsively when faced with authority figures or rules. Similarly, if we witnessed impulsive behaviour being rewarded or praised in our past, we may have internalized those behaviours as acceptable or effective.

Society often places expectations and pressures on us, and when we perceive a deviation from these norms, it can trigger impulsive responses. For instance, if we feel judged or criticized for not conforming to societal standards, we may react impulsively to defend ourselves or seek approval.

Moreover, impulsive reactions can also be influenced by our core beliefs and values. These deep-rooted convictions shape our perception of the world and ourselves. If we hold rigid beliefs that prioritize

CHALLENGE IMPULSIVE THOUGHTS

immediate gratification or self-preservation above all else, we are more likely to engage in impulsive behavior. These beliefs can stem from personal experiences, cultural influences, or even biological factors.

Furthermore, certain psychological factors can contribute to impulsive reactions. Conditions such as attention deficit hyperactivity disorder (ADHD) or borderline personality disorder (BPD) are characterized by impulsivity as a core symptom. These conditions may result from a combination of genetic, neurological, and environmental factors, making us more prone to impulsive thoughts and behaviours.

When examining the roots of impulsive reactions, it is essential to consider the role of our emotions. Emotions play a significant role in influencing our thoughts and actions. Strong emotions, including anger, fear, or excitement, can override our rational thinking processes, leading to impulsive behaviour. Understanding our emotional triggers and learning to regulate our emotions can help mitigate impulsive reactions.

Examining the roots of impulsive reactions involves exploring the interplay of various factors. Our conditioning, learned behaviours, social and cultural influences, core beliefs, psychological factors, and emotional responses all contribute to impulsive thoughts and behaviours. By gaining insight into these underlying causes, we can develop strategies to manage and reframe our automatic reactions more effectively. Through self-reflection, therapy, and personal growth, we can gradually reduce the influence of impulsive thinking and make more deliberate and reasoned choices in our lives.

Our past experiences play a significant role in shaping our thoughts, behaviours, and reactions, including impulsive thinking. When examining impulsive thoughts, it becomes crucial to delve into our personal history and explore the events that may have influenced our automatic reactions.

Past experiences can create patterns of thinking that contribute to impulsive thoughts. If someone has experienced a series of negative or traumatic events, they may develop a pessimistic outlook on life. This negative outlook can lead to impulsive thoughts including assuming the worst in every situation or jumping to conclusions without considering alternative explanations.

Similarly, childhood experiences and upbringing can shape impulsive thinking. Those of us who grew up in an environment where our opinions were consistently dismissed or invalidated may develop impulsive thoughts of self-doubt or a constant need for validation from others. These thought patterns can impact decision-making processes and result in impulsive behaviors seeking immediate approval or validation.

Moreover, past failures or setbacks can also contribute to impulsive thinking. If someone has experienced repeated disappointments or rejections, they may develop a fear of failure or a sense of urgency to act quickly without considering the potential consequences. This fear can lead to impulsive thoughts including taking unnecessary risks or making hasty decisions without careful deliberation.

Understanding how past events shape impulsive thinking allows us to gain insight into our automatic reactions. By identifying the specific experiences that have influenced our thought patterns, we can begin to challenge and reframe those thoughts in a more constructive manner.

One effective approach is to engage in reflective exercises or therapy that encourages exploring past events and their impact on current thought processes. This exploration can help us identify any negative or limiting beliefs that have emerged from their past experiences. Once these beliefs are recognized, we can work towards reframing them by seeking evidence to challenge their validity.

By examining and unpacking past experiences, we can gain a deeper understanding of the root causes behind impulsive thoughts. This understanding provides a foundation for personal growth and allows us to develop more balanced and rational thinking patterns. It enables us to break free from the limitations imposed by past events and empowers us to make more informed decisions based on the present circumstances rather than automatic reactions rooted in the past.

Cognitive restructuring is a powerful technique that helps us challenge and reframe our automatic reactions and impulsive thoughts through logical examination. It involves examining the underlying assumptions and beliefs that contribute to impulsive thinking and replacing them with more rational and balanced alternatives. By engaging in cognitive restructuring, we can gain greater control over our thoughts and make more informed and constructive decisions.

Cognitive restructuring is being aware of the automatic reactions and impulsive thoughts that arise in various situations. This requires mindfulness and attentiveness to one's own thinking patterns. By paying close attention to the thoughts that emerge, we can begin to identify the underlying beliefs and assumptions that drive our impulsive reactions.

Once these automatic thoughts and underlying beliefs are identified, the next step is to critically examine their validity. This involves questioning the evidence supporting these thoughts and considering alternative explanations and perspectives. It is important to challenge the accuracy and fairness of these thoughts and consider whether they are based on facts or distorted perceptions.

One effective technique in cognitive restructuring is called "evidence gathering." This involves systematically collecting evidence that supports or refutes the automatic thoughts and beliefs. By evaluating the strength and reliability of this evidence, we can gain a clearer understanding of the accuracy of our initial reactions. This process helps to counteract cognitive biases and encourages a more balanced and objective assessment of the situation.

Additionally, we can use logical reasoning to reframe our automatic reactions. This involves identifying any logical errors or cognitive distortions in our thinking, including overgeneralization, jumping to conclusions, or catastrophizing. By challenging these distorted thinking patterns, we can replace them with more realistic and rational thoughts.

It is essential to replace the automatic reactions with alternative and more balanced thoughts. This can be achieved by generating alternative explanations or interpretations of the situation. By considering different perspectives, we can broaden our understanding and develop more flexible thinking patterns. This process encourages us to consider the possibility of positive outcomes, potential solutions, or alternative ways of perceiving the situation.

Furthermore, cognitive restructuring involves practicing and reinforcing the new rational thoughts. This requires repetition and consistency to strengthen the neural pathways associated with the revised thinking patterns. Over time, we can develop a habit of questioning our automatic reactions and replacing them with more reasoned and balanced thoughts.

Developing rational thinking is a crucial step in challenging impulsive thoughts and reframing automatic reactions. Impulsive thoughts often stem from distorted thinking patterns and cognitive biases that lead to irrational beliefs and actions. By cultivating a more rational and balanced mindset, we can gain greater control over our impulsive thoughts and make more informed decisions.

One of the key aspects of developing rational thinking is learning to recognize and challenge cognitive distortions. Cognitive distortions are habitual patterns of thinking that skew our perception of reality. Cognitive distortions include black-and-white thinking (seeing things as either all good or all bad), overgeneralization (drawing broad conclusions based on limited evidence), and personalization (assuming excessive responsibility for events that are beyond our control). By becoming aware of these distortions, we can begin to question their validity and replace them with more accurate and balanced thoughts.

CHALLENGE IMPULSIVE THOUGHTS

Cultivating rational thinking is learning to separate facts from interpretations and assumptions. Our minds often generate automatic thoughts based on limited information and personal biases. These thoughts can be highly subjective and may not align with objective reality. By critically examining the evidence and seeking alternative explanations, we can gain a more balanced perspective on a situation. This involves asking ourselves questions like, "What evidence do I have to support this thought?" and "Are there other possible explanations for this situation?"

Developing rational thinking entails adopting a more flexible and open-minded attitude. It involves acknowledging that our initial perceptions and judgments may not always be accurate or complete. By actively seeking alternative perspectives and considering different viewpoints, we can broaden our understanding of a situation and challenge our impulsive thoughts more effectively. This can be achieved through techniques such as perspective-taking, where we attempt to put ourselves in someone else's shoes and see things from their point of view.

Furthermore, developing rational thinking involves honing critical thinking skills. This includes the ability to analyze information objectively, identify logical fallacies, and evaluate the reliability and validity of sources. By applying critical thinking, we can approach our impulsive thoughts with skepticism and examine them in a more logical and rational manner. This process often involves asking questions like, "What evidence supports this thought?" and "Is this thought based on facts or assumptions?"

Ultimately, developing a more rational and balanced mindset requires practice and patience. It is a skill that can be cultivated through consistent effort and self-reflection. By challenging impulsive thoughts and reframing automatic reactions, we can gain greater control over our decision-making process and lead more fulfilling and meaningful lives.

In our daily lives, we often make assumptions and hold beliefs without consciously examining their validity. These automatic thoughts can contribute to impulsive reactions, as they may be based on limited information, biased perspectives, or past experiences that no longer hold true.

When faced with impulsive thoughts or reactions, it is crucial to take a step back and examine the underlying assumptions that fuel them. Assumptions are often deeply ingrained in our thinking patterns and can influence our behaviour without us realizing it. By questioning our assumptions, we can challenge their accuracy and uncover any cognitive distortions that may be present.

To begin questioning assumptions, it is helpful to identify the thoughts or beliefs that are driving our impulsive reactions. These thoughts may manifest as inner dialogue, self-talk, or mental images that accompany the impulsive behavior. Once we have identified these automatic thoughts, we can subject them to scrutiny.

One effective strategy for evaluating the validity of our automatic thoughts is to gather evidence both for and against them. This involves examining the facts and considering alternative explanations or interpretations of the situation. By engaging in this process, we can gain a more balanced perspective and reduce the influence of impulsive thinking.

It is also essential to examine the emotional content associated with our automatic thoughts. Emotions can often cloud our judgment and lead to biased thinking. By acknowledging and understanding the emotions underlying our impulsive thoughts, we can evaluate whether they are appropriate responses to the situation at hand.

Another useful technique in questioning assumptions is to seek external input. Sharing our automatic thoughts and beliefs with trusted individuals can provide valuable insights and alternative viewpoints.

CHALLENGE IMPULSIVE THOUGHTS

Others may challenge our assumptions by offering different perspectives or additional information that we may not have considered.

In addition to external input, we can also engage in self-reflection and introspection. Taking the time to explore our own cognitive biases, preconceived notions, and personal experiences can help us recognize any patterns or tendencies that contribute to impulsive thinking. By gaining self-awareness, we can actively work towards overcoming these biases and developing more rational thought processes.

By engaging in the process of questioning assumptions, we can develop a more nuanced understanding of ourselves and the world around us. We can become more aware of the biases and cognitive distortions that influence our impulsive thinking and take steps to correct them. Through this introspective journey, we can cultivate a more rational and balanced mindset, leading to better decision-making and improved overall well-being.

In the process of challenging impulsive thoughts and reframing automatic reactions, it is crucial to explore alternative perspectives. Our impulsive thoughts are often based on a limited or biased view of a situation, and by seeking alternative interpretations and viewpoints, we can gain a more comprehensive understanding of the situation at hand.

One way to seek alternative perspectives is by considering different viewpoints from others. This involves actively seeking out the opinions and insights of people who may have a different outlook or experience related to the situation. By listening to their perspectives, we can broaden our own understanding and challenge any preconceived notions or biases that may be influencing our impulsive thoughts.

Another approach is to engage in self-reflection and introspection. This involves taking a step back from the immediate emotional response triggered by impulsive thoughts and examining the situation from a more objective standpoint. By questioning our assumptions and considering alternative explanations, we can uncover different ways of interpreting the situation.

Additionally, it can be helpful to explore different sources of information. In the age of abundant information and diverse media platforms, it is important to critically evaluate the sources we rely on and seek out alternative viewpoints. By exposing ourselves to a range of perspectives, we can challenge our own biases and gain a more nuanced understanding of the situation.

It is worth noting that seeking alternative perspectives does not mean discarding our own beliefs or values. Rather, it is an exercise in expanding our understanding and considering different possibilities. By engaging in this process, we can challenge the rigidity of our impulsive thoughts and develop a more flexible and open-minded approach to interpreting the world around us.

To effectively seek alternative perspectives, it is essential to cultivate curiosity and a willingness to learn. This involves being open to new ideas and actively seeking out opportunities to engage with diverse viewpoints. It may also be beneficial to engage in activities that promote empathy and understanding, including reading literature from different cultures or engaging in discussions with others who hold differing opinions.

Hence, seeking alternative perspectives is a valuable tool in challenging impulsive thoughts and reframing automatic reactions. By exploring different viewpoints, considering alternative interpretations, and actively seeking out diverse perspectives, we can break free from the limitations of our impulsive thoughts and develop a more balanced and nuanced understanding of the world. This process encourages personal growth, critical thinking, and the cultivation of empathy, ultimately leading to more rational and informed decision-making.

Impulsive thoughts often arise from hasty judgments and automatic reactions without careful consideration. To counteract these impulsive tendencies, it is crucial to develop problem-solving strategies that engage critical thinking. By employing this approach, we can navigate challenging situations more effectively and make informed decisions.

Problem-solving begins with recognizing that impulsive thoughts may not always lead to the best outcomes. It may involve taking a step back from immediate reactions and actively engaging in a logical thought process. This first requires identifying the specific problem or situation at hand. By clearly defining the issue, we can focus our efforts on finding an appropriate solution rather than succumbing to impulsive responses.

Once the problem is defined, it is essential to gather relevant information. This includes considering the context, gathering facts, and seeking different perspectives. Taking the time to gather information allows us to gain a comprehensive understanding of the situation, which can help in generating more thoughtful and well-informed responses. It also helps in challenging any preconceived notions or biases that may influence impulsive thoughts.

With a solid understanding of the problem and adequate information, critical thinking can be applied to generate potential solutions. This involves thinking creatively and considering multiple alternatives. By brainstorming various possibilities, we can explore a range of perspectives and outcomes. It is important to suspend judgment during this stage and maintain an open mind to all potential solutions, even if they initially seem unconventional or contrary to impulsive thoughts.

Once a list of potential solutions is generated, it is time to evaluate their feasibility and potential consequences. Critical thinking plays a crucial role in this evaluation process. Each solution should be carefully assessed based on its practicality, effectiveness, and potential impact on oneself and others. This evaluation requires a balanced and rational mindset, free from the influence of impulsive thoughts or emotions. It is important to objectively weigh the pros and cons of each solution and consider the long-term implications rather than being swayed by immediate gratification.

After careful evaluation, the most appropriate solution can be selected. This decision should align with one's values, goals, and desired outcomes. It may require compromise or finding a middle ground that satisfies multiple factors. By engaging in critical thinking, we can make well-reasoned decisions that are less likely to be driven by impulsive thoughts or emotions.

Implementing the chosen solution is the final step in problem-solving. It is essential to develop a plan of action that outlines the necessary steps to be taken and any potential challenges or obstacles that may arise. By having a well-thought-out plan, we can maintain focus and stay on track, reducing the likelihood of succumbing to impulsive thoughts or distractions along the way.

Throughout the problem-solving process, it is important to remain mindful and self-aware. Regularly reflecting on one's thoughts and actions can help identify any recurring impulsive tendencies and provide an opportunity for course correction. By practicing critical thinking and problem-solving strategies consistently, we can gradually overcome impulsive thoughts and develop a more rational and balanced approach to decision-making.

In this empowering chapter on challenging impulsive thoughts, we have embarked on a journey of self-discovery and transformation. By examining and reframing our automatic reactions, we have gained valuable insights into the nature and impact of impulsive thoughts, paving the way for positive change and personal growth.

Understanding impulsive thoughts has allowed us to unravel the intricate web of influences that shape our lives. We have recognized that impulsive thoughts can have significant consequences on our well-being and decision-making. By acknowledging their presence and impact, we

CHALLENGE IMPULSIVE THOUGHTS

have taken the first step toward regaining control and living a more intentional and fulfilling life.

Identifying automatic reactions has been a crucial aspect of our journey. We have developed the ability to recognize the triggers that elicit impulsive thoughts, enabling us to break free from their grip. By bringing conscious awareness to our automatic reactions, we have empowered ourselves to respond in a more deliberate and thoughtful manner.

Examining the roots of our impulsive reactions has been a transformative process. We have delved deep into our past experiences, uncovering the underlying causes that fuel impulsive thinking. Through self-reflection and introspection, we have gained valuable insights into the patterns and triggers that perpetuate impulsive thoughts, empowering us to challenge and transform them.

Unpacking past experiences has allowed us to understand the ways in which they shape our thought patterns. We have embraced the opportunity to heal past wounds, release limiting beliefs, and reframe our perspectives. By revisiting and reframing our past experiences, we have opened the door to personal growth and the possibility of a more positive and empowered future.

The role of emotions in influencing impulsive thoughts has become evident. We have learned to navigate the complex interplay between emotions and impulsive reactions, recognizing that emotions can often cloud our judgment. Through self-awareness and emotional regulation, we have developed the capacity to respond to challenging situations with greater clarity and rationality.

Cognitive restructuring has been a powerful tool in reframing automatic reactions. We have challenged the validity of our impulsive thoughts, examining them through a logical lens. By consciously questioning and reshaping our automatic reactions, we have empowered ourselves to adopt more balanced and constructive perspectives

Developing rational thinking has been a cornerstone of our transformation. We have cultivated a mindset rooted in reason and critical thinking, enabling us to approach situations with clarity and objectivity. By embracing rationality, we have unlocked the potential to make more informed decisions and navigate life's challenges with greater wisdom and resilience.

Questioning assumptions has opened the door to expanded possibilities. We have recognized the limitations of our automatic thoughts and beliefs, challenging their validity and exploring alternative perspectives. By fostering a mindset of curiosity and openness, we have embraced the richness of diverse viewpoints, enriching our understanding of the world and ourselves.

Problem-solving strategies have become our allies in overcoming impulsive thoughts. We have harnessed the power of critical thinking to identify creative solutions and navigate obstacles. By employing problem-solving techniques, we have discovered new paths, empowered ourselves to overcome challenges, and embraced a mindset of growth and resilience.

As we conclude this chapter, let us celebrate the progress we have made in challenging our impulsive thoughts. By examining and reframing our automatic reactions, we have reclaimed our agency, fostered personal growth, and cultivated a more intentional and purposeful life. We now possess the tools and insights to navigate life's complexities with greater wisdom, resilience, and positivity. Let us embrace this newfound awareness and continue our journey toward a life filled with mindful choices, empowered decisions, and a sense of inner peace.

CHALLENGE IMPULSIVE THOUGHTS

CHAMPION *Your* THOUGHTS

What are thoughts? We all have them and they travel with us as long as we are awake. We cannot run away from them as they live in us. They are fed by what we see, hear, smell, taste, and touch. They are affected by our emotions, depending on what we are thinking. Some say we live in the conscious mind and maintain our livelihood are by opinions, beliefs, perceptions, and ideas gathered from the five senses that are part of the hosting of our well-being.

Thoughts allow us to make sense of the world we live in and what we experience. It allows us to interpret what we see, hear, feels, smell, and taste. Thoughts are modifiable elements that we can change with the information gathered from our attitude, belief, environment, experience, skills, and education. Thoughts are determined through negative and positive thinking patterns which can affect a our mental and emotional well-being. Negative thoughts can cause and fill our lives with stress, anxiety, justification, and anger which can become overwhelming to bear. Positive thoughts do the opposite, they bring us into the light, instead of darkness, and strengthen our mental and emotional health.

We can be in control of our thoughts and can stop them from taking a detour to the destruction of our lives. When a thought comes to the mind, the mind has the choice to store it in its memory depending on how important it is to the person. If the thoughts are associated with an event of the past that already exists in our memory, then it will stir up an emotion that was registered with that thought. The current thought will become a stimulant that will bring the past thought alive. The memory associated with that emotion will create a world of thoughts that were associated with that past thought creating a web of thoughts, which we find ourselves trapped inside.

As an example, imagine you were walking down the street with your eyes on your cell phone. You were not paying attention to anyone but your phone. In your peripheral vision, your eye picked up a male figure on the other side of the street talking to someone. You are not really paying any attention, except the fact that he is wearing a red t-shirt. You come home to your partner or spouse or some friends or family member. It's around dinner time, and usually every day there is a routine when you come home. You may join your partner, friends, or family to watch a show before dinner or relax with a snack. Most of the time you will all cook together or decide on eating out or ordering in. Your usual routine would be to go to the kitchen to see if food is made and grab a snack. Today was one of those days you went to the kitchen expecting snacks or a meal. But you notice there is dirty glass in the sink and a few dirty pots and pans on the stove. This was not unusual, however, a wave of anger rose from the inside and you took the dirty glass and smash it on the floor saying "you have been home all day, why is there nothing to eat and dirty dishes in the kitchen?" Although the routine was not abnormal, there was a burst of anger which was unexpected.

As a psychological assessment is completed, the person getting angry recall his day and his journey home. The only unusual thing that happened that day was man on the opposite side of the road wearing a red t-shirt. What is unusual about this is the fact that when you were about six years old, you were sexually abused by an older person wearing a red t-shirt that looks similar to what the man was wearing. The figure of the person looked the same, yet you did not pay any attention to the man with the red t-shirt. A memory card was triggered with an underlining unresolved issue. As the memory card got triggered, anger was released affecting your mental and psychological well-being. In simple words, we need to resolve unresolved issues, as they can be triggered anytime anywhere like a time bomb as they are retained in mind.

All thoughts revolve around one major thought and are created and developed from the amount of attention we give them. A single thought can expand to multiple thoughts if we don't contain it. Thoughts feed from any of our sensory nerves, especially what we hear and what we see. They get energy from whatever is connected to our five senses that have relevance to our thoughts. The dominant thought likes to be the center of attention which will justify every idea that comes to the mind to stay in control and be fed.

We all make decisions consciously or subconsciously without thinking. We all have impulsive reactions when provoked, and depending on the topic, we can even become defensive and rude. We need to give ourselves time to process a thought before impulsively answering, especially when the thought is a trigger to us. We all have regrets for things we say, mistakes we wish never happened, and the flaws and weaknesses that we present. Although it is difficult to admit it, we are not perfect. Our imperfections are seen through our thought processes and how we vocalize issues and solutions. When we are able to process any friction or give ourselves time to ponder what we collide with, we will have a better resolution. We will have less stress while cleaning up the mess we created when we allow our minds to think about what we heard and dissect it before concluding how we feel.

Individuals struggling with their mental health conditions, addictions, and psychological traumas carries multiple thoughts in their mind. Those with addiction issues think of all the reasons to justify their use with the main thought "this will be the last time." Those with anxiety may struggle from a thought that is triggered by an abusive relationship or a traumatic event. Those with psychosis could have a thought stuck in their mind, and feel pressured to act on the thought, especially if it is being driven by command hallucinations.

Words we hear can trigger an unfavorable memory created in the past. Words have a tendency to look for other words to form a sentence, particularly negative words. Our brain will search for every word that connects to statements or situations and formulate a sentence. When we have unresolved situations, our brain looks for a vocabulary of words to express feelings. When we recondition the mind, we gain the power to flush out negative words and experiences, and replace them with positivity. Individuals struggling with depression or a mood disorder only perceive darkness, and as a result, develop a pessimistic approach which leads to hopelessness and suicidal thoughts. When a person is able to change their thought process and implement positive words, they can turn on the 'optimism' switch in the mind. Nevertheless, every dark room has a light switch, we just need to find it.

Everyone has the power to stop negative thinking from learned therapies. The mind needs to be distracted, even for thirty seconds. For example, during your work hours, you may develop a need to use the washroom and on your way to the washroom, you may meet someone. You spend about ten minutes talking to them about something and your mind switches the thought of the need to use the washroom to another topic. You may not end up going to the washroom after that conversation as the mind may forget where you were going. However, in a short while, your thought of wanting to go to the washroom will return.

Another example would be driving down the street and smelling food. Although you may have had a meal earlier, the smell of food triggers the brain. Same as seeing someone eat ice cream, someone with a coffee or a burger. Once our sensory nerves are triggered, we develop urges or cravings. Unhealthy urges and cravings can lead to bigger issues. That's why we need to develop a habit of being able to distract our thoughts even for thirty seconds if we want to rewire the brain. This small habit of processing our thoughts will make a huge difference in our lives.

We could be watching a television commercial advertising a coconut cream pie or fried chicken and suddenly we develop urges or cravings desiring it and want it right away. Just like watching an advertisement for cars, trucks, clothes, and so on. If we have a buying habit, we will make an online purchase, or head down to the store to satisfy the craving. Several people purchase clothes from window shopping, or what they see others wearing, especially if it is of a popular brand or worn by someone who is a celebrity.

Thoughts are more prominent in the mind just before falling asleep. And, depending on the nature of the thoughts, we could be stuck with a thought or developed racing thoughts. Thoughts will eventually become like a movie playing in the mind, especially if they are thoughts accumulated during the day by a disagreement or a regret. We have to learn how to manipulate thoughts, creating distractions or diversion thoughts which this workbook will teach.

Thoughts can affect your eating habits, your sleeping patterns, concentration, memory, and other daily functions. They can spiral down into depression and anxiety. We all tend to look for coping strategies that will work quickly, which usually are negative. Gambling, alcohol, street drugs, misuse of prescription medications, and self-harm are usually the choices for a quick fix. But this workbook teaches other ways that are positive and healthy. Moreover, you will also learn how to take advantage of your disadvantage and implement strategies that help you to gain control of your thoughts, instead of your thoughts leading you.

Taking control of the thought is the first step to strengthening the mind and re-training your thinking patterns. Positive thinking is the second step to reconditioning the mind and becoming optimistic even in the storms of life. Re-phrasing what you think or restructuring your thoughts is the third step to bring healing to your emotional life. And, living for what you assume to be fruitful is the fourth step to carry you to be a champion over your thoughts.

We need to champion our thoughts. We need to remind ourselves that champions are not born; they are made. We need to look at ways to become champions over our thoughts in order to conquer our addictions, anxieties, and depression. Champions use their weakness as strengths, they use their regrets, mistakes, and hurts as fertilizer to fertilize their future, they push hard to overcome their weakness, they strive to win and are not easily distracted, and they are competitive and do not give room for failure. We need to strive towards being a champion over our thoughts if we want to move out of the pit of feeling low and depressed. We must see the light at the end of the tunnel, the light switch on the wall of a dark room. We must see the anchor that will sustain us from drifting in the sea of life. We must see the bigger picture of our lives, where we want to be, where we can be, and what would it take to get there.

Champions look at the worse situation that could have happened and remind themselves that there are worse situations than theirs. They look at where they are in life and where they would want to be. They tell themselves exactly what they want to hear. They have mastered the concept of enjoying who they are. They feel comfortable dating themselves and falling in love with who they see in the mirror. They don't rely on others to add value and worth to their lives, nor are they co-dependent on others. Champions are confident that life has much to offer if they take the necessary steps to reach their goals.

We are all champions if we chose. It means we need to practice gaining control, train ourselves to be the best, think positively, and be optimistic about life. When a thought comes that has no bearing of fruitfulness, we should not waste time entertaining them. Some of us may have thoughts including "I feel like a failure," "nobody understands me," and "what's the purpose of my life anyway." We need to recondition the mind with "I am not a failure," "I don't need others to understand me," "My life has purpose and value" and "I have a bright future waiting for me to discover with family and friends" "I love the gift of life and admire the person I see in the mirror." We flush our minds with positive affirmations and the tools in this book will help with distractions and diversions to see the value and worth we carry as a person.

Championing our thoughts does not mean that we will have no more negative thoughts. We will be surprised to know negative thoughts are a normal part of our thinking process and even from birth, our brain is hardwired to be more negative as we develop picking up information like a sponge from all those around us. As we grow up, whatever have tainted the mind, control our thinking and regulates our thoughts. The problem that arise when we failed to control our negative thoughts, is the fact that they consume us mentally, emotionally and psychologically. Our lives become miserable, and we become victim to a number of mental disorders.

Not all mental or psychological issues originates from negative thinking, but they can stem from them. Negative thoughts can be responsible for how we process what we feel without exploring options to be in control. We need to eradicate all negative thinking before the thoughts consumes us, leaving us bitter, angry, frustrated, and miserable with ourselves.

It can be a challenge to stay positive when life is full of problems that are overwhelming and stress related. differentiate between negative thinking and worries that leads to stress. We need to program ourselves that negativity will lead us to depressive symptoms and create lack of motivation. It will affect how we function on a day-to-day level at the workplace, with the family, at home and our own personal life. We will not feel like we could achieve anything and give up without even trying. We will be sad, angry, and exhausted with does not work well together. We will see the entire world around us being the problem than seeing that changes need to come from in the inside out. Some of us may get sick from allowing negativity to percolate like coffee. We must learn to identify negative thoughts and work towards conditioning the mind to stay positive, regardless of life's situation. There is always light at the end of the tunnel, be the first to see it.

With a positive outlook in mind, we can gain determination, confidence, and willpower to achieve desired results. Whereas with a negative outlook, even the smallest task seems difficult and a challenge for us to pursue.

Many of us are often afraid of the future developing anxiety. We need to champion the way we think to be in control of not allowing unnecessary thoughts to fill our mind. We are often afraid of the unknown and unsure of what the future holds for us. This often leads to failure in the mind when there is no motivation to pursue goals. No matter how we look at it, worrying about the future is a waste of time and energy, and it leads to negative thinking. The key to getting rid of these negative thoughts is to acknowledge that there is a limitation as to what we can do and what we cannot do. The ultimate goal is to focus on taking baby steps and not setting goals that we are unable to meet. This will help avoid unnecessary disappointments.

We all make mistakes from time to time, as we are not perfect. We all have flaws and does things that we have regrets. We all say things we are ashamed of, but people with a negative mindset tend to focus more on past mistakes, flaws, failures and regrets than others. We have to remind ourselves that we are not perfect and that's okay. When we acknowledge that we have flaws and failures and regrets we wish we can change, we need to work on avoiding making the same mistakes twice. We want to focus on staying positive and not allowing our minds to go down the rabbit hole where we isolate ourselves from others. We cannot change the past, but we can change the future.

We all have responsibilities in life like everyone else, especially financially. And, in order to grow up and mature we need to take on the responsibility of being financially stable. There are times when things can go against our financial plans and expectations, creating worry and fear. We have to remind ourselves there are no shortcuts to life. If we don't work hard, we will never have enough money to survive without living from paycheck to paycheck. We may suffer financial instability when we find it difficult to settle at a job or chose a career path, when there is spending habit, we find difficult to control, lack of resources, and lack of motivation to go back to school and educate ourselves with a proper education. A lack of financial stability brings negative thinking to the mind as some of us may not be able to past the thought we need to change and not the system. If we believe we can work less and gain more money, we need a plan. We believe in the get rich quick scheme we will soon learn it does not work. If we believe we have a product to see or go on self-employed we need to make sure we understand it may take some time before the business blossom. We need to convince the mind that we have a blueprint, a plan for our future to avoid financial instability.

We should not allow our confidence level to speak for us and make unwise decisions. Usually lack of confidence can manifest itself in control, frustration and anger. We may think we are never good enough; we cannot do what we put our minds to do, there are more qualities than us and we love hope. We could be an introvert or extrovert we all can struggle with confidence issues, which leads to negative thinking. We have to mind ourselves that confidence can only grow when we lead the principles of developing our skills, knowledge and experience. The more we practice our growing in our areas of weaknesses, the more our confidence level will increase. Sometimes we may need to bluff our way in a situation for confidence to manifest itself. You assume you don't have the skills to do the job. You cannot fulfill your potential. Our lack of confidence can also be responsible for low self-esteem which leads to negative thinking.

Thinking and worrying about something is normal but the real problem arises when this type of thinking becomes continuous. So many of us can be over thinkers, where we may have a bad experience or someone may have said something to us and we hold on to that thought over and over again. We have to replace negative thoughts with someone positive. We have to remind ourselves that we cannot change a person or what they think, but we can change how we accommodate them. We have to avoid our minds from thoughts that are destructive as the thoughts will become our impulsive thoughts which will be a challenge to break. Overthinking can result from regrets and wrong choices we made in the past regarding education, career, employment, family dynamics, relationships, marriages, social lifestyles, spirituality, financial and other psychosocial issues. Moreover, overthinking is believed to be the primary cause of negative thinking resulting in severe mental problems including depression, anxiety and psychosis. Overthinking can affect our psychological well-being leading to negative thinking and unrealistic expectations.

We all can set unrealistic expectations for ourselves, relationships, family and friends, parenting, career and employment, education, and budgeting. We need to be realistic when we set a goals for our lives. We need to be realistic otherwise we will become more frustration which leads to negative thinking. Several of us who set unrealistic or unachievable goals find ourselves through processing our thoughts to engage in negative thinking. We want to avoid losing self-confidence and motivation to become an achiever. We need to focus on that which we know is our destiny for our lives and avoid blaming others for our wrong choices or bad decision we make.

It is very easy to blame ourselves or others when negative things occurs, like spending money and not having enough left over to pay the bills, getting involved in a automobile accident, losing a love one from an unexpected incident. Very often when something negative happens in our lives we blame ourselves or others instead of accepting the mistake and moving forward. We cannot replace a jar when it falls to the ground and break, so why blame. Like the old saying "why cry over spilled milk." We need to work on resolutions, otherwise we get the blaming concepts to manifest itself through negative thinking which is manifested through unhealthy choices.

Living a unhealthy lifestyle is really a choice, even though there would not be a lot of people who would not agree. We all love to eat from time to time, and in our western culture we have so many fast food that makes it easy accessible for buy. Some of us may eat out of convenience when we are hungry and others out of cravings. As much as we can manage our intake of illicit drugs, alcohol, and negativity from others we could also manage unhealthy living. Unhealthy living is not just wrong choices of food intake, it is the lifestyle we choose to live. It may mean avoiding exercising, socializing, developing spirituality, positive thinking, and the places and things that we are addicted to. Anything we do that will harm ourselves is considered unhealthy. We need to take pride in who we are and the value and worth we carry as a person. Unhealthy living brings regrets which creates negative thinking.

Our emotions and thoughts can have a significant impact on our physical health and how we function as a person. Living in freedom where we avoid judge it ourselves and others can relief a lot of unnecessary weight on our shoulders. Negative thinking builds stress and other psychological issues that can weigh us down. It can drain us emotionally where we are like a well without the flow of water. We feel exhausted and find it difficult to relax or even have fun with others. Furthermore, negative thoughts can influence our relationships, marriages, academic performance, work life, and socializing. They also affects our path to a happy and successful life. Negative thinking affects our psychological well-being.

Fortunately, there are many scientifically proven ways that provide an effective solution to negative thinking which are evidence-based. To live a happy and well-balanced life we have to learn how to dance to the sounds of life. We need to learn how to recondition the mind and restructure our thinking. We need to flush out the negativity to positivity. There are many tips to do so, however we need to become aware of the change we need to make otherwise it will not happen. We need to implement changes that will benefit our mental and spiritual wellbeing. We should learn how to catch ourselves and create new neuropathways that are of a positive nature. It will not be an easy task, but it will be worth it at the end, when others compliment us of the changes they see. When we learn to live happy, calm and peaceful internally, it will manifest itself externally.

We all to learn the healthy stimulants is good for the brain. A change of environment can do this for us. We have to know that it is okay to develop a distance between toxic people and still maintain a relationship with them. Our minds are fed like our stomach with the environment we live in. It can be what goes on at work, social media we view, the music we listen to, the movies we watch, the news, who we have as role models or blueprints in our lives, and those who influence us. It's like the dog who had several pops. The dog was hit by a car which left her with a broken leg. She was not helped and walked with a limp. All her puppies walked with a limp as they thought their mother's way of walking was the right way.

Another healthy stimulant is physical activity which helps develop dopamine's and serotonins. Going for walks, the gym, exercising, excursions, tours, getting involved in a sport, running, bird watching, people watching, window shopping, photography, scrapbooking etc. Anything that involves physical activity will stimulate the brain through the five sensory nerves, releasing dopamine's and serotonins. This is our stress relievers that will help maintain happiness. We need to incorporate at lease thirty minutes a day to something that can involve physical activity, it will help with our anxiety level.

Talk therapy has always been part of human nature. When we talk to someone, we can feel like a weight has left us. It is difficult to find trustworthy people, hence it is important to find therapist. So many of us struggle to talk about our concerns, our feelings and things that bothers us. Yet talking to someone has helped millions of people around the world. People pay a lot of money to share their thoughts with professionals, where they can empty their mind and find ways to fill it with healthy thoughts. There are certain people who will come across your life where you can develop a trust to share certain things that bothers you. Nothing is wrong in getting a second opinion. Sometimes our pride prevents us from talking to others as we believe we have the answer or we know it all. We could never know it all; we could never have the answers to all of the struggles we go through and burying our feelings under the rug will cause us to stumble and fall flat on our faces. We burn a lot of bridges when we keep everything inside and live a superficial shallow life. Directly and indirectly things that bothers us will only exacerbates if we keep it inside our mind. We will overthink or we will bury them which will be triggered by others with similar incidents or encounters. Some religious group finds it easy to talk to someone and share their heart, some talk to God, some talk to a friend, some a therapist and others themselves. We need to talk to someone about deep issues or incidents that has occurred to avoid bigger problems as we age.

Another important healthy stimulant is learning to volunteer our time in humanitarian aid. It is important to do some form of humanitarian work. People who help others develop a happiness internally with words that they themselves cannot explain. Most hospitals, libraries, shelters, foodbanks, churches, orphanages, and supporting the less fortunate started with volunteers. Life is about giving, what can we do for others instead of what we can get from others. When we do something for others, we will soon realize that there are others in worse cases than us. Sometimes we may believe that our issues of life is worse and no one can ever understand, until we start helping others. Feeding the poor, help build a house in a third world country, volunteer at a shelter, give donations to the less fortunate, visit an orphanage, go on a mission trip somewhere and you will be in awe of the problems people deal with. We would appreciate what we have and who we are very quickly.

Learn to be grateful for everything in life, the little things and the big things. The fact that we have life, treat it like there is no tomorrow. Treat others with respect and dignity like today is the last day you will see them. Developing gratitude and showing how grateful you are will open doors to people's hearts, including yours. Gratefulness keeps us humble and focused on being positive. It's difficult to be grateful and be negative. When we are fighting negativity, it's easy to forget all the positive things in our lives, making it a challenge to be grateful.

Keeping a journal of our feelings and emotions is a good way to empty the mind. We all should be keeping a log of our day on a journal; this will help with getting rid of negative thoughts. We need to write down our feelings and emotions and how others have impacted our lives in a positive way. Taking ten to fifteen minutes a day will be like medicine to the soul. Keeping a log will show our progress and will help with a determination of having a healthy thought process. We would want to generate more positive thoughts than negative thoughts on our notebook, therefore we will become more mindful on controlling what we think.

Mindfulness techniques, meditation, deep breathing, relaxation exercises, and various other self-awareness methods help us to control our emotional reactions to situations. We need to learn how to smell the imaginary rose and blow out the imaginary candle when overwhelmed and is in a anxious mode. They allow our minds to take over our thought processes. Practicing mindfulness contribute to the ability to use our thoughts more adaptively with fewer negative thoughts. There are a lot of teaching on mindfulness, meditation, diaphragmic breathing and other self-awareness methods that helps reduce negative thinking.

We need to identify our thoughts in order to rule them out. When we identify our thoughts and note down, we can evaluate their cause for floating around our minds. As we watch our thoughts and identify them, we will be able to regulate them and replace them with positive thoughts. Although it is not as simple to replace negative thoughts with positive thoughts, identifying the cause of negative thoughts will get us to the root. And, when we can remove the negative roots and replant positive ones, we can have healthy thoughts. We will need to work on willpower, self-control, and mindfulness techniques to remain calm when we feel triggered with this process. With that being said, some thoughts are activated because we have not put closure to an incident.

It is important to bring closure to incidents or situations that creates negative thinking. There are many ways to bring closure to the past that is affecting the future. We need to replace the negative memory card with positive memory card. We may need to write down our past on paper and burn it with a celebrate so the brain identifies an ending to the past as a celebration. We would draw the past in an image form in the mind and place them in a mirror, breaking them to pieces where they no longer exist as a whole in image in the mind, replacing the pieces with a new image in the mind. We could put the past in a bottle and see it float away from you. There are lots of closure suggestions that can be implemented to rid of the negative thinking. When we chose to do so, we will create new habits that will be healthy, protecting our minds from the battle is goes through from thinking negatively.

New habits are like learning a language or writing with the less dominant hand. It takes time but has positive results at the end. Instead of trying to overcome negative thought patterns, try to replace them with new habits. We need to turn our attention from harmful thinking to a healthy lifestyle that we can enjoy. Begin with something simple, easy, and most importantly, something you really enjoy that will take your mind off negative thoughts.

The following chapters will share about some of the causes that affects our mental health, which is not necessary a demon as some may believe. We have to understand that there is a cause for everything in life, including some of who are struggling with our mental health. A healthy spiritual life is the key to have which can give us insight and wisdom who to target the root cause of issues that are responsible for our mental health.

MASTER *Your* EMOTIONS

When considering the concept to "Rewire Your Brain," we need to explore the profound realm of emotions, unlocking the transformative potential they hold. Our emotions are a vibrant tapestry woven into the fabric of our daily lives, influencing our thoughts, actions, and overall well-being. By understanding and mastering our emotions, we gain the power to shape our lives in extraordinary ways.

Throughout this chapter, we will embark on an enlightening exploration, equipping ourselves with invaluable tools to navigate the vast spectrum of emotions. We will begin by unravelling the intricate role that emotions play in our daily experiences. By recognizing their significance, we lay the foundation for a deeper understanding of ourselves and those around us.

Negative emotions can often be challenging to navigate. We need to be guided in identifying and managing these emotions, empowering ourselves to transcend our grasp. Additionally, we will unveil the transformative practice of cultivating emotional awareness and regulation, fostering a harmonious balance within.

Embracing empathy and compassion is a powerful force that not only transforms our own lives but also has a profound impact on the lives of others. We will explore how to cultivate these qualities within ourselves, nurturing a sense of connection and fostering healthier relationships.

We will uncover the immense power of positive emotions and gratitude, illuminating the path towards a more joyous and fulfilling existence. Moreover, we will delve into constructive approaches to managing anger and frustration, ensuring that these emotions serve as catalysts for personal growth.

Fear and anxiety may at times feel overwhelming, but we will learn how to overcome their grip. Developing emotional resilience becomes a cornerstone of our emotional well-being, empowering us to bounce back from adversity and embrace life's challenges with unwavering strength.

In this chapter, we place a special emphasis on enhancing emotional intelligence—an essential skill that allows us to navigate the complex landscape of emotions with finesse. By sharpening our emotional intelligence, we expand our capacity for self-awareness, empathy, and effective communication.

We recognize the immense power of emotional bonds and relationships in shaping our lives. By strengthening these connections, we foster a supportive network that uplifts and inspires us on personal growth and fulfilment.

By rewiring our brain to harness the power of our emotions, we unlock a world of endless possibilities. Let us embark on this exhilarating voyage and unlock the potential for a truly extraordinary life.

Emotions are the vibrant colours that paint the canvas of our daily experiences, shaping our perceptions, decisions, and interactions with the world. They are an essential part of what makes us human, providing valuable insights into our inner landscape. Understanding the role of emotions in our lives is the first step towards harnessing their transformative power.

Emotions serve as a guiding compass, alerting us to what matters most to us and influencing the choices we make. They offer a rich tapestry of information about our needs, desires, and values. For instance, feeling joy may indicate that we are engaging in activities that bring us fulfilment, while sadness might signal a need for reflection or change. By paying attention to our emotions, we gain valuable self-awareness and can make more informed decisions aligned with our authentic selves.

Moreover, emotions play a crucial role in our relationships and social interactions. They serve as a universal language, allowing us to connect with others on a deep level. Empathy, for instance, relies on our ability to recognize and resonate with the emotions of those around us. By understanding our own emotions, we develop the capacity to relate to others more effectively, fostering stronger bonds and healthier connections.

In addition, emotions influence our cognitive processes and overall well-being are an outlet for mastering our emotions. Our emotions can impact our attention, memory, and problem-solving abilities. Positive emotions, such as gratitude and joy, have been linked to increased creativity, resilience, and overall life satisfaction. Conversely, prolonged negative emotions, like stress or anger, can have detrimental effects on our mental and physical health.

To truly understand the role of mastering our emotions in our daily life, it is essential to cultivate emotional awareness and master our emotions. This involves developing a non-judgmental and curious attitude towards our own emotional experiences. By observing and reflecting on our emotions, we gain valuable insights into their triggers and patterns, empowering us to respond in more adaptive and constructive ways.

Negative emotions can often feel like a heavy burden, weighing us down and clouding our perspective. However, knowledge and techniques can identify and effectively manage these emotions, allowing us to regain control and foster a more positive outlook on life.

Before we can effectively manage negative emotions, it is crucial to understand their underlying causes and the purpose they serve. Negative emotions including sadness, anger, fear, and frustration are natural responses to various life situations. They can signal unmet needs, indicate areas of growth, or act as protective mechanisms. By gaining a deeper understanding of these emotions, we can approach them with compassion and curiosity.

Identifying negative emotional patterns is an essential step towards managing them effectively and mastering our emotions. Through self-reflection and mindfulness, we can learn to recognize recurring negative emotions and the triggers that set them in motion. This self-awareness allows us to intervene at an early stage, preventing these emotions from spiralling out of control.

Acceptance is a powerful tool in managing negative emotions and master our emotions. It involves acknowledging and validating our emotions without judgment or resistance. By embracing our feelings and being emotionally honest with ourselves, we can create a safe space for self-exploration and growth. This practice allows us to move beyond the initial emotional response and work towards finding constructive solutions.

Discovering healthy coping strategies is essential for managing negative emotions and mastering our emotions. We will explore a range of techniques, including deep breathing exercises, meditation, journaling, and physical activity, that can help us regulate our emotions and find inner calm. These strategies provide practical and accessible ways to navigate challenging emotions, fostering resilience and emotional well-being.

Negative emotions are often fuelled by negative thought patterns. We must challenge and reframe these thoughts, replacing them with more positive and constructive perspectives. By reshaping our mindset, we can transform negative emotions into opportunities for growth and self-empowerment.

Practicing self-compassion is a crucial component of managing negative emotions and master our emotions. We need to cultivate kindness and understanding towards ourselves, allowing us to embrace our vulnerabilities and mistakes without self-judgment. Self-compassion provides a solid foundation for emotional well-being and enables us to navigate negative emotions with gentleness and resilience.

By mastering the identification and management of negative emotions, we reclaim the power to shape our emotional landscape. With the tools and insights provided we can develop the skills necessary to transform negative emotions into catalysts for personal growth, paving the way towards a more fulfilling and joyful life.

Emotional awareness and regulation is another option of mastering our emotions. We have fundamental skills that empower us to navigate the intricate landscape of our emotions with grace and wisdom.

Emotional awareness involves tuning in to the subtle cues and signals our emotions send, allowing us to gain valuable insights into our inner world. By cultivating emotional awareness, we develop a profound sense of self-awareness, enabling us to discern the underlying causes and triggers of our emotions. It is the ability to recognize, understand, and acknowledge our emotions as they arise.

To cultivate emotional awareness, it is crucial to create a space of mindfulness and reflection. This involves setting aside dedicated time to tune in to our emotions, exploring how they manifest within our bodies, minds, and hearts. Through practices like meditation, journaling, or simply taking quiet moments for self-reflection, we can observe our emotions without judgment, gently exploring their depths and learning from their messages.

Emotional regulation goes hand in hand with emotional awareness and master our emotions, as it involves the conscious management and modulation of our emotions. When we have a deep understanding of our emotional landscape, we gain the power to respond to our emotions in a way that aligns with our values and goals.

One powerful technique for emotional regulation is mindfulness. By practicing mindfulness, as discussed earlier we cultivate a non-judgmental awareness of our emotions in the present moment, allowing us to observe them without getting carried away by their intensity.

Mindfulness helps us create a space between our emotions and our responses, enabling us to choose more constructive and balanced reactions.

We must develop healthy coping mechanisms. These are activities and practices that help us regulate our emotions in a positive and constructive manner. Examples of healthy coping mechanisms include engaging in physical exercise, practicing relaxation techniques, seeking support from trusted friends or professionals, or engaging in creative outlets such as art, music, or writing.

Furthermore, cultivating emotional awareness and regulation includes developing emotional intelligence, which involves the ability to recognize and understand not only our own emotions but also the emotions of others. By enhancing our emotional intelligence, we become more adept at interpreting and empathizing with the emotions of those around us, which strengthens our capacity for effective emotional regulation and interpersonal relationships.

Cultivating emotional awareness and regulation and mastering our emotions, is essential in approaching ourselves with kindness, compassion, and patience. It's not about striving for perfection but rather about embracing our emotions as valuable messengers guiding us towards personal growth and well-being. By cultivating emotional awareness and regulation, we gain the transformative power to navigate life's challenges with resilience, grace, and authenticity.

Another area of mastering our emotions is cultivating empathy and compassion has become more important than ever. These profound qualities have the power to bridge gaps, dissolve barriers, and create a kinder, more harmonious society. By practicing empathy and compassion, we not only enhance our own well-being but also contribute to the well-being of others, making a lasting impact on the world around us.

Empathy is the ability to understand and share the feelings of others, stepping into their shoes and seeing the world through their eyes. It is a skill that allows us to connect deeply with others, fostering understanding, acceptance, and support. When we cultivate empathy, we break down the walls of judgment and criticism, embracing the diversity of human experiences which includes compassion.

Compassion is the genuine desire to alleviate the suffering of others. It goes beyond understanding and extends to taking positive action. Compassion enables us to extend a helping hand, offer support, and show kindness to those who are in need. It is a force that drives us to make a difference, one act of kindness at a time.

Practicing empathy and compassion begins with developing self-awareness which helps us to master our emotions. By understanding our own emotions and experiences, we become more attuned to the feelings and needs of others. It allows us to cultivate a deep sense of empathy, appreciating the challenges and triumphs that shape individuals' lives.

Active listening plays a vital role in empathy and compassion. When we truly listen, without judgment or interruption, we create a safe space for others to express themselves. By validating their emotions and experiences, we foster a sense of belonging and connection, nurturing the bonds that bring us together.

Empathy and compassion are not limited to personal relationships; they extend to the larger community and even beyond. Engaging in acts of kindness, volunteering, or supporting charitable causes allows us to practice compassion on a broader scale. It reminds us of our interconnectedness and the impact we can have on the lives of others, making a positive difference in the world.

Practicing empathy and compassion also requires us to cultivate self-compassion. Just as we extend kindness and understanding to others, we must learn to be gentle and forgiving with ourselves. Embracing self-compassion allows us to navigate life's challenges with resilience and grace, fostering a sense of well-being from within.

As we develop and deepen our empathy and compassion, we become catalysts for positive change. Our actions ripple through our immediate circles, inspiring others to embrace these qualities. Together, we create a compassionate ripple effect, transforming our communities and fostering a more compassionate and understanding world. By practicing empathy and compassion, we not only nurture our own growth but also contribute to a brighter and more compassionate world while mastering our emotions.

Positive emotions are like rays of sunshine that brighten our lives, uplifting our spirits and enhancing our overall well-being. They have the power to reshape our perspectives, infusing every moment with a sense of joy and contentment.

To nurture positive emotions, it is crucial to develop an awareness of the present moment. Often, we find ourselves caught up in the hustle and bustle of daily life, focusing on future goals or dwelling on past regrets. However, by bringing our attention to the present, we open ourselves to experience the beauty and wonder that surrounds us.

One powerful technique to nurture positive emotions is practicing mindfulness. As discussed earlier by cultivating a non-judgmental awareness of our thoughts, feelings, and sensations, we become more attuned to the present moment. Mindfulness allows us to savour the simple pleasures, finding joy in the smallest of things—a blooming flower, a gentle breeze, or a shared laugh with a loved one.

Mastering our emotions includes the concept of gratitude, which is like a radiant flame, that has the ability to ignite a profound transformation within us. It is the practice of acknowledging and appreciating the abundance in our lives, both big and small. Gratitude opens our hearts to the richness of our experiences, fostering a deep sense of contentment and fulfilment.

To nurture gratitude, we can start by keeping a gratitude journal. Each day, we reflect upon the blessings and positive aspects of our lives, jotting them down with heartfelt appreciation. This simple act of writing, helps us shift our focus from what is lacking to what is abundant, cultivating a mindset of abundance and gratitude.

Expressing gratitude to others is a powerful practice that nurtures positive emotions, mastering it. By acknowledging and appreciating the contributions and kindness of others, we strengthen our connections and foster a culture of gratitude. Whether through a heartfelt thank-you note, a kind gesture, or a sincere word of appreciation, our expressions of gratitude have the power to uplift not only ourselves but also those around us.

Engaging in activities that bring us enjoyment and fulfilment is another effective way to nurture positive emotions. These activities can be as diverse as pursuing a hobby, spending time in nature, engaging in creative expression, or simply connecting with loved ones. By intentionally incorporating these activities into our lives, we create opportunities for moments of pure bliss and fulfilment.

As we embrace the practice of nurturing positive emotions and gratitude, we will begin to witness a profound transformation in our lives. We will develop a greater resilience in the face of challenges, as positive emotions act as a buffer against stress and adversity. Our relationships flourish as we radiate joy and appreciation, creating a positive ripple effect in our interactions with others. With practice and intention, we can cultivate a life brimming with joy, contentment, and an unwavering sense of gratitude. Embark on this transformative path, savouring the beauty of each moment and cultivating a radiant heart filled with positivity and appreciation.

Mastering our emotions would include an understanding of anger and frustration. These are natural emotions that everyone experiences from time to time. While these emotions can be powerful, they also have the potential to be destructive if not managed effectively. We need to rewire our brain to manage anger and frustration. There are strategies and techniques for harnessing the energy of anger and frustration, transforming them into constructive forces for personal growth and positive change.

It is crucial to develop self-awareness when it comes to anger and frustration. Understanding the triggers, patterns, and physical sensations associated with these emotions allows us to intercept them before they escalate. By recognizing the early signs of anger and frustration, we can employ proactive measures to address them in a healthy manner.

One key aspect of managing anger and frustration constructively is learning effective communication skills. Often, these emotions arise when our needs are not being met or when conflicts arise in our relationships. By developing assertive communication skills, we can express our feelings and concerns in a calm and respectful manner, fostering understanding and resolution.

We must practice emotional regulation and self-soothing. When anger or frustration arises, taking a moment to pause, breathe deeply, and engage in calming activities such as meditation, journaling, or physical exercise can help diffuse the intensity of these emotions. This enables us to approach situations with a clearer and more composed mindset, promoting better decision-making and problem-solving.

Moreover, cultivating empathy and perspective-taking can greatly assist in managing anger and frustration constructively. By stepping into the shoes of others and seeking to understand their viewpoints and experiences, we can foster compassion and open-mindedness.

This not only helps us find common ground and resolve conflicts more effectively but also cultivates empathy within ourselves, promoting a more harmonious and understanding mindset.

In addition, exploring the root causes of our anger and frustration can provide valuable insights into our deeper needs and desires. Sometimes, these emotions may be masking underlying feelings of hurt, fear, or insecurity. By addressing and healing these underlying issues, we can reduce the intensity and frequency of anger and frustration in our lives.

Furthermore, adopting a proactive problem-solving approach can channel the energy of anger and frustration into positive action. Instead of allowing these emotions to fester and lead to destructive behaviours, we can use them as fuel to identify and address the core issues at hand. This proactive mindset empowers us to find creative solutions and make constructive changes in our lives.

Ultimately, managing anger and frustration constructively requires patience, practice, and a willingness to embrace personal growth. It is an ongoing journey of self-discovery, self-reflection, and self-mastery. By transforming our relationship with these emotions, we unlock the potential to create a more peaceful and fulfilling existence, fostering healthier relationships and personal well-being. Anger and frustration need not control us. Instead, we can harness their fiery energy and use it to ignite positive transformation within ourselves and the world around us. By managing these emotions constructively, we step into our power and embrace the limitless possibilities of personal growth and positive change.

Fear and Anxiety is another area of mastering our emotions. They may feel overwhelming, but with the right mindset and tools, we can navigate through them and reclaim our sense of peace and confidence. This will help us master our minds. Fear and Anxiety often arise from distorted thinking patterns and negative self-talk. Cognitive restructuring involves identifying and challenging these unhelpful thoughts and replacing them with more realistic and positive ones. By consciously reframing our thoughts, we can gradually shift our mindset and reduce the intensity of fear and anxiety.

If certain situations or stimuli trigger fear or anxiety, it can be helpful to expose ourselves to them gradually and systematically. Start with small, manageable steps and gradually increase exposure over time. As we repeatedly face our fears in a controlled and supportive manner, we can desensitize ourselves and build confidence in our ability to cope.

Learning and practicing relaxation techniques can be instrumental in managing fear and anxiety. Deep breathing exercises, progressive muscle relaxation, guided imagery, and meditation are just a few examples of techniques that can help calm our minds and bodies, reducing the intensity of fearful and anxious feelings.

When intrusive or negative thoughts fuel fear and anxiety, employing the thought-stopping technique can be beneficial. Whenever we notice an unhelpful thought arising, mentally shout "Stop!" or imagine a stop sign. Then, consciously replace that thought with a positive affirmation or a calming image.

Building emotional regulation skills allows us to respond to fear and anxiety in a more controlled and constructive manner. Techniques including identifying and labelling emotions, practicing self-soothing strategies, and engaging in activities that promote relaxation and emotional well-being can help us navigate through challenging emotions effectively.

Developing self-compassion is vital when facing fear and anxiety. We need to treat ourselves with kindness and understanding, acknowledging that these emotions are a natural part of being human. Offer ourselves words of encouragement and practice self-care during difficult moments. Remember that it's okay to ask for help and support when needed.

When fear and anxiety become overwhelming, engaging in activities that shift our focus can provide temporary relief. Pursue hobbies, spend time with loved ones, immerse yourself in creative endeavours, or engage in physical exercise. These positive distractions can help redirect our attention and provide a sense of relief from anxious thoughts.

If fear and anxiety persist and significantly impact your daily life, seeking professional support from a therapist or counsellor can be invaluable. These professionals can provide specialized guidance, teach you additional coping skills, and help you navigate the underlying causes of your fears and anxieties.

We need to be patient and compassionate with ourselves as we navigate these emotions. It takes time and practice to develop new habits and coping mechanisms. By embracing courage, utilizing these strategies, and seeking support when needed, we can gradually overcome fear and anxiety, reclaim our inner strength, and live a life guided by empowerment and serenity.

Another area of mastering our emotions is emotional resilience, which refers to the ability to adapt and bounce back from challenging or stressful situations. It involves the capacity to effectively manage and regulate one's emotions, maintain a positive outlook, and cope with adversity in a healthy manner. Developing emotional resilience is crucial for overall well-being and mental health, as it enables us to navigate life's ups and downs with greater ease and emotional stability.

To cultivate emotional resilience, several key strategies can be employed. First and foremost, self-awareness is essential. This involves recognizing and understanding our own emotions, thoughts, and triggers. By being aware of our emotional state, we can begin to develop a deeper understanding of our own reactions and responses to various situations. This self-awareness serves as the foundation for building emotional resilience.

Connecting with others who provide a sense of safety, understanding, and empathy can be immensely helpful in times of stress or hardship. Friends, family, or even support groups can offer emotional support and provide a sounding board for our thoughts and concerns. Additionally, seeking professional help, including therapy or counselling, can also be beneficial in developing emotional resilience.

Developing effective coping strategies is an important component of emotional resilience. These strategies may include engaging in regular physical exercise, practicing mindfulness or meditation, engaging in hobbies or activities that bring joy and fulfilment, and developing healthy ways to manage stress. By incorporating these practices into our daily routine, we can enhance our ability to cope with adversity and maintain emotional well-being.

Furthermore, cultivating a positive mindset is vital in developing emotional resilience. Fostering optimism and a belief in our ability to overcome challenges can significantly contribute to emotional strength. This involves reframing negative thoughts, focusing on strengths and positive aspects of a situation, and practicing gratitude. By cultivating a positive outlook, we can build resilience and navigate difficulties with a greater sense of optimism and hope.

Developing emotional resilience is crucial for maintaining mental health and well-being. By practicing self-awareness, building a support system, developing effective coping strategies, and fostering a positive mindset, we can enhance our ability to adapt and thrive in the face of adversity. Building emotional resilience is an ongoing process that requires time, effort, and self-reflection, but the benefits are significant in terms of overall emotional well-being.

Improving emotional intelligence enhances our skills in mastering our emotions. It advances our ability to understand, manage, and express emotions effectively. Tapping into our emotional intelligence includes paying attention to our own emotions, thoughts, and behaviours. We need to reflect on our reactions in various situations and try to identify patterns. We should consider keeping a journal to track our emotions and gain insights into our triggers and responses.

Engage in mindfulness meditation or other practices that promote present-moment awareness. This can help us develop a non-judgmental attitude toward our emotions, allowing us to observe and understand them better.

We need to share empathy as it helps us to understand and share the feelings of others. Practice active listening by giving our full attention to others when they speak, and try to put ourselves in their shoes. Show genuine interest and concern for their emotions and experiences.

Effective communication is crucial for emotional intelligence. Practice expressing yourself clearly, assertively, and respectfully. Pay attention to nonverbal cues such as body language and tone of voice. Additionally, learn to actively listen and validate the emotions of others.

Emotional intelligence involves effectively managing our own emotions and stress levels. We need to develop healthy coping mechanisms for stress, including exercise, deep breathing, and engaging in activities we enjoy. Take breaks when needed and prioritize self-care to maintain emotional balance.

Resilience allows us to bounce back from setbacks and challenges.

We can build our resilience by reframing negative situations, focusing on solutions rather than dwelling on problems, and seeking social support when need.

Ask trusted friends, family members, or colleagues for feedback on your emotional intelligence. Their perspectives can help you gain insights into blind spots or areas for improvement.

Look for workshops or seminars that focus on emotional intelligence or related topics. These interactive sessions can provide opportunities for skill-building and personal growth.

Regularly set aside time to reflect on your emotions, interactions, and personal growth. Ask yourself how you could have handled certain situations better and what lessons you can learn from them.

Remember that improving emotional intelligence is a journey that takes time and practice. By consistently working on these skills, we can enhance our emotional intelligence and cultivate more meaningful relationships, both personally and professionally.

Mastering our emotions requires us to strengthen our emotional bonds in relationships. Building and nurturing strong emotional bonds in relationships is essential for our overall well-being and happiness. Meaningful connections with others provide us with a sense of belonging, support, and fulfilment.

Effective communication is the foundation of any strong relationship. It involves both expressing ourselves honestly and actively listening to others. By practicing active listening, we demonstrate genuine interest and empathy, allowing others to feel heard and understood. Open and honest communication fosters trust and creates a safe space for both parties to express their thoughts, feelings, and needs.

Providing emotional support develops strong emotional bonds in relationships. It involves being there for others during challenging times and celebrating their successes. It requires empathy, compassion, and a willingness to offer comfort and encouragement. By showing understanding and offering a listening ear, we can strengthen emotional bonds and demonstrate our commitment to the relationship.

Spending quality time together is crucial for building emotional bonds. It involves dedicating focused and undivided attention to the other person. This could be engaging in activities or conversations that both individuals enjoy, creating shared experiences and memories. Quality time helps foster a deeper connection and reinforces the importance of the relationship.

Trust is a fundamental aspect of strong emotional bonds. It involves being reliable, consistent, and keeping our commitments. Additionally, being vulnerable with each other creates a deeper sense of trust. By sharing our authentic selves, including our fears, insecurities, and dreams, we invite others to do the same, strengthening the emotional connection.

Conflicts are a natural part of any relationship. Strengthening emotional bonds requires developing healthy conflict resolution skills. This includes addressing issues openly and respectfully, actively listening to each other's perspectives, and seeking compromise or win-win solutions. By resolving conflicts in a constructive manner, we can prevent resentment and build a stronger foundation for the relationship.

Small acts of kindness and expressions of appreciation can go a long way in strengthening emotional bonds. Simple gestures like offering a helping hand, expressing gratitude, or surprising the other person with something they value can demonstrate care and reinforce the importance of the relationship.

Respecting and accepting others for who they are is vital for building emotional bonds. This involves recognizing and valuing their individuality, beliefs, and choices. By fostering an environment of respect and acceptance, we create a safe space where both individuals can freely express themselves, fostering trust and deepening the emotional connection.

Finding common goals and interests helps to strengthen emotional bonds. Engaging in activities together, pursuing shared hobbies, or working towards a common purpose can create a sense of unity and teamwork. It allows both individuals to support and encourage each other, leading to a stronger emotional bond.

In any relationship, forgiveness plays a crucial role. Holding onto grudges and past hurts can erode emotional bonds. Learning to forgive and let go of resentment is essential for healing and moving forward. By practicing forgiveness, we create space for growth, understanding, and a deeper connection with the other person.

Regularly checking in with each other ensures that the relationship remains a priority. It involves having open and honest conversations about the state of the relationship, individual needs, and any concerns. Regular check-ins allow us to address issues promptly, make necessary adjustments, and strengthen the emotional bond.

In conclusion, mastering your emotions is a transformative journey that can bring immense positivity and fulfilment into our lives. Throughout this chapter, we have explored various aspects of emotional well-being, providing our with valuable insights and practical strategies to enhance our emotional intelligence.

Understanding the role of emotions in daily life is the first step towards creating a harmonious inner world. By acknowledging and accepting the full spectrum of our emotions, we empower ourselves to respond to life's challenges with clarity and wisdom.

Identifying and managing negative emotions is an essential skill that enables us to navigate through difficult situations with grace and resilience. By practicing self-awareness and adopting healthy coping mechanisms, we can transform negative emotions into opportunities for growth and self-improvement.

Cultivating emotional awareness and regulation empowers us to make conscious choices in how we respond to both internal and external stimuli. Through mindfulness practices and self-reflection, we can develop a greater sense of emotional balance and stability, allowing ourselves to maintain a positive outlook even in the face of adversity.

Practicing empathy and compassion towards others is not only beneficial for our relationships but also for our own emotional well-being. By seeking to understand and support others, we cultivate a deep sense of connection and create a positive ripple effect that spreads kindness and positivity.

Nurturing positive emotions and gratitude is a powerful way to uplift our spirits and enhance our overall well-being. By focusing on the good in our lives and cultivating gratitude for even the smallest blessings, we invite more positivity and joy into our daily experiences.

Managing anger and frustration constructively is a skill that can significantly improve our relationships and personal growth. By learning to express and channel these intense emotions in healthy ways, we can maintain healthy boundaries and build bridges of understanding and collaboration.

Overcoming fear and anxiety requires courage and resilience. It is a crucial step towards personal growth and fulfilment. By challenging limiting beliefs and adopting helpful coping strategies, we can break free from the grip of fear and anxiety, opening up a world of possibilities and personal transformation.

Developing emotional resilience is a lifelong process that equips us with the tools to bounce back from setbacks and navigate life's challenges with grace and strength. By building a strong support system, practicing self-care, and cultivating a growth mindset, we can develop the resilience necessary to thrive in the face of adversity.

Improving emotional intelligence is a continual journey of self-discovery and self-improvement. By enhancing our ability to understand and regulate emotions, empathize with others, and effectively communicate, we can navigate relationships and life's complexities with greater ease and authenticity.

Finally, strengthening emotional bonds in relationships is a cornerstone of emotional well-being. By investing time and effort into nurturing meaningful connections with loved ones, we create a support network that sustains and uplifts us through life's highs and lows.

Remember, mastering your emotions is a lifelong endeavour, and it requires patience, self-compassion, and consistent practice. As we integrate the insights and strategies from this chapter into our lives, we will embark on a transformative journey towards emotional well-being, leading to a more fulfilling and joyful existence. Embrace this journey wholeheartedly, and may your newfound emotional mastery bring you boundless happiness and peace.

FEED and FUEL *Your* BRAIN

The brain, with its intricate network of billions of neurons, is a marvel of nature. It controls our thoughts, emotions, memories, and every action we take. Just like any other organ in our body, the brain requires proper nourishment to function optimally. It thrives on a delicate balance of nutrients, vitamins, minerals, and hydration to perform its intricate tasks seamlessly.

In "Feeding and Fuelling the Brain," we will embark on an enlightening journey, shedding light on the vital role that nutrition plays in brain health. We will explore how incorporating brain-boosting foods into our diet can enhance cognitive abilities, and how striking the right balance of macronutrients can unlock our brain's full potential. This enhances our ability to "Rewire Your Brain."

Beyond the traditional understanding of nutrition, there is a fascinating realm of the gut-brain connection. The intricate interplay between the gut microbiome and the brain has garnered significant attention, highlighting how the health of our digestive system directly impacts our mental well-being.

Additionally, we often overlooked the essential factor of hydration. Discovering how maintaining optimal hydration levels can significantly impact our brain performance and cognitive function, allowing us to unlock greater mental clarity and focus.

No discussion on brain health would be complete without delving into the role of vitamins, minerals, and antioxidants. There are specific nutrients that are crucial for our brain function. By understanding how these micronutrients interact with the brain, we can gain valuable knowledge to make informed dietary choices that support cognitive well-being.

Sleep, another pillar of our brain health, deserves our utmost attention. We need to emphasize the importance of restorative sleep and its profound impact on our brain function. Unveiling the mysteries of sleep, we can explore its role in memory consolidation, emotional regulation, and overall mental resilience.

Managing caffeine and alcohol consumption should be an opened discussion, as these substances have a notable influence on our cognitive abilities. By understanding the effects of these stimulants and depressants, we will be empowered to make conscious choices that support our cognitive well-being.

Brain-enhancing supplements and nootropics are also another area we need to explore to understand how we can rewire our brain what we feed and fuel it. While these substances hold promise in enhancing cognitive performance, we need evidence-based insights to help navigate this complex landscape and make informed decisions regarding their use.

The choices we make can positively impact our brain's health and reshape our cognitive abilities for the better. By understanding the profound connection between nutrition, hydration, sleep, and brain function, we hold the key to unlocking our brain's true potential.

Proper nutrition plays a crucial role in maintaining optimal brain health and cognitive function (Smith, J., & Johnson, A., 2022). The brain is a highly metabolic organ that requires a constant supply of energy and nutrients to function efficiently. The food we consume provides the necessary building blocks and fuel for the brain to carry out its complex processes.

Antioxidants are compounds that help protect the brain from oxidative stress and damage caused by free radicals (Jones, B., et al., 2020). Examples of antioxidants include vitamins C and E, beta-carotene, and flavonoids found in colourful fruits and vegetables, such as berries, citrus fruits, spinach, kale, and broccoli.

Choline is a nutrient that plays a vital role in brain development, learning, and memory (Davis, S., et al., 2018). It is a precursor to acetylcholine, a neurotransmitter involved in cognitive function. Foods rich in choline include eggs, liver, soybeans, fish, and cruciferous vegetables.

The Mediterranean diet, characterized by high consumption of fruits, vegetables, whole grains, fish, olive oil, and moderate intake of red wine, has been associated with a reduced risk of cognitive decline and neurodegenerative diseases (Johnson, R., et al., 2019). This dietary pattern provides a variety of nutrients and antioxidants that support brain health and may help protect against age-related cognitive decline.

Chronic inflammation can negatively impact brain health and contribute to cognitive decline (Adams, K., et al., 2021). A diet high in processed foods, refined sugars, unhealthy fats, and low in nutrient-dense foods can promote inflammation. On the other hand, an anti-inflammatory diet, rich in fruits, vegetables, whole grains, healthy fats (e.g., olive oil, avocados, nuts), and lean proteins, can help reduce inflammation and support brain health.

Emerging research has highlighted the importance of the gut-brain axis, the bidirectional communication system between the gut and the brain (Williams, M., et al., 2023). The gut microbiota, the trillions of bacteria residing in our digestive system, play a crucial role in this communication. A healthy gut microbiota, supported by a diverse and fiber-rich diet, can positively influence brain function and mental well-being.

Overall, maintaining a balanced and nutrient-dense diet, rich in brain-boosting foods, is essential for promoting brain health and optimizing cognitive function throughout life (Smith, J., & Johnson, A., 2022). A healthy diet, combined with regular exercise, adequate sleep, and mental stimulation, forms the foundation for a healthy brain.

Eating a well-balanced diet that includes brain-boosting foods can have a significant impact on our cognitive function and overall brain health. Omega-3 fatty acids are essential for brain health and development. They have been linked to improved cognitive function and a reduced risk of age-related cognitive decline. Fatty fish like salmon, mackerel, and sardines are excellent sources of omega-3s. If we follow a vegetarian or vegan diet, we can opt for plant-based sources such as flaxseeds, chia seeds, and walnuts.

Berries, such as blueberries, strawberries, and blackberries, are rich in antioxidants and other compounds that have been shown to improve brain function. They help reduce inflammation and oxidative stress, which are associated with age-related cognitive decline. We can enjoy berries on their own, add them to smoothies, or sprinkle them on top of cereals or yogurt.

Dark chocolate with a high cocoa content (70% or more) contains flavonoids, which have antioxidant and anti-inflammatory properties. These compounds can improve blood flow to the brain and enhance cognitive function. However, it's essential to consume dark chocolate in moderation due to its calorie and sugar content.

Leafy greens like spinach, kale, and broccoli are packed with nutrients that support brain health. They are rich in vitamins, minerals, and antioxidants, including vitamin K, lutein, folate, and beta-carotene. These nutrients have been linked to improved cognitive function and a reduced risk of dementia.

Turmeric is a spice commonly used in Indian cuisine and contains a compound called curcumin. Curcumin has potent antioxidant and anti-inflammatory properties and has shown promise in improving memory and reducing the risk of neurodegenerative diseases. You can incorporate turmeric into your diet by adding it to curries, soups, or smoothies.

Whole grains, such as brown rice, quinoa, oats, and whole wheat bread, provide a steady supply of glucose to the brain, its main energy source. They also contain fiber, which helps regulate blood sugar levels and maintain stable energy throughout the day. Opting for whole grains over refined grains can promote better cognitive function and long-term brain health.

Nuts and seeds, including almonds, walnuts, pumpkin seeds, and sunflower seeds, are excellent sources of antioxidants, healthy fats, vitamin E, and other nutrients that support brain health. These foods have been associated with improved memory and cognitive function.

It's important to note that while incorporating brain-boosting foods into our diet can be beneficial, they should be part of an overall balanced eating plan. Variety and moderation are key to obtaining a wide range of nutrients that support brain function. Additionally, it's best to consult with a healthcare professional or registered dietitian for personalized dietary advice tailored to your specific needs and health conditions.

Balancing macronutrients, which are the essential nutrients required in large quantities, is crucial for promoting optimal cognitive function and supporting brain health. The three primary macronutrients are carbohydrates, proteins, and fats. Each of these macronutrients plays a vital role in providing energy, supporting neurotransmitter function, and maintaining overall brain health. Here's a closer look at how each macronutrient affects cognitive function:

Carbohydrates are the primary source of energy for the brain. When consumed, carbohydrates are broken down into glucose, which is used as fuel by the brain cells. Complex carbohydrates, such as whole grains, fruits, and vegetables, provide a steady release of glucose, promoting stable energy levels and sustained cognitive function. It's important to choose healthy, unprocessed carbohydrates and avoid refined sugars that can lead to energy crashes and impair cognitive performance.

Proteins are essential for the synthesis of neurotransmitters, the chemical messengers that facilitate communication between brain cells. Neurotransmitters like dopamine, serotonin, and norepinephrine play a crucial role in regulating mood, focus, and memory. Including high-quality protein sources like lean meats, fish, eggs, dairy products, legumes, and nuts in your diet can help provide the necessary amino acids for neurotransmitter production, supporting optimal cognitive function.

Healthy fats are integral to brain health as they make up a significant portion of the brain's structure and help insulate and protect nerve cells.

Balancing these macronutrients in our diet is key to maintaining optimal cognitive function. It's important to note that individual dietary needs may vary based on factors such as age, activity level, and overall health. Consulting with a healthcare professional or a registered dietitian can provide personalized guidance to ensure we're meeting our specific macronutrient requirements for optimal brain health.

In addition to macronutrients, it's also crucial to pay attention to micronutrients, including vitamins and minerals, as they play a vital role in supporting brain function. Adequate intake of essential vitamins and minerals like vitamin B12, folate, vitamin D, magnesium, and zinc is essential for optimal cognitive function. A well-balanced diet that includes a variety of nutrient-dense foods is the best way to ensure you're getting the necessary macronutrients and micronutrients to support your brain health.

The gut-brain connection refers to the bidirectional communication pathway between the gastrointestinal (GI) tract and the central nervous system (CNS), which includes the brain and spinal cord. This intricate connection is mediated through a complex network of nerves, hormones, and biochemical signalling pathways. Emerging research has highlighted the significant influence of the gut microbiota, a diverse community of microorganisms residing in the GI tract, on brain function and overall mental well-being.

The gut microbiota plays a crucial role in maintaining the health and function of the digestive system. However, recent studies have shown that the microbiota can also impact brain function. The gut microbiota produces various neurotransmitters, including serotonin, dopamine, and gamma-aminobutyric acid (GABA), which are involved in regulating mood, cognition, and behaviour. Imbalances in the gut microbiota composition, known as dysbiosis, have been linked to neurological conditions such as anxiety, depression, and even neurodegenerative diseases.

The gut-brain axis is the communication system that enables the bidirectional flow of information between the gut and the brain. It involves several pathways, including the vagus nerve, immune signalling molecules, and microbial metabolites. The vagus nerve serves as a major communication highway, relaying signals between the gut and the brain. Additionally, the gut microbiota can release metabolites, such as short-chain fatty acids (SCFAs), that can enter the bloodstream and affect brain function.

The composition of the gut microbiota is influenced by various factors, including genetics, environment, and notably, diet. A diet rich in fiber and diverse plant-based foods promotes the growth of beneficial gut bacteria and helps maintain a healthy microbiota. On the other hand, a diet high in processed foods, added sugars, and saturated fats can lead to an imbalance in gut microbial communities, potentially impacting brain health.

The gut-brain connection has been implicated in the development and management of mental health disorders. Research suggests that certain psychiatric conditions, such as anxiety and depression, are associated with alterations in gut microbiota composition. Manipulating the gut microbiota through dietary interventions, probiotics, or fecal microbiota transplantation (FMT) has shown promise in improving symptoms of these conditions.

Maintaining a healthy gut microbiota is crucial for optimizing brain function. Strategies to support a healthy gut microbiota include consuming a diverse and balanced diet rich in prebiotic foods (e.g., fruits, vegetables, whole grains), which provide nourishment for beneficial gut bacteria. Probiotics, which are live microorganisms that confer health benefits when consumed, can also be incorporated through fermented foods or supplements. However, it's important to note that research on specific strains and their effects on brain health is ongoing.

Understanding and harnessing the gut-brain connection opens up exciting possibilities for promoting brain health and potentially managing neurological disorders. Further research is needed to elucidate the mechanisms involved and to develop targeted interventions that can modulate the gut microbiota for therapeutic purposes. In the future, personalized approaches to nutrition and the gut-brain axis may play a key role in optimizing cognitive function and mental well-being.

Hydration plays a crucial role in maintaining optimal brain function.

The brain is composed of about 75% water, and even mild dehydration can have a significant impact on cognitive abilities.

Dehydration can impair various aspects of cognitive function, including memory, attention, concentration, and overall mental performance. Studies have shown that even mild dehydration, as little as 1-2% loss in body weight due to fluid loss, can lead to cognitive decline.

Adequate hydration is essential for maintaining the structure and function of brain cells. Water helps to regulate the balance of electrolytes in the brain and facilitates the transport of nutrients and oxygen to brain cells. It also aids in the removal of metabolic waste products, toxins, and excessive neurotransmitters.

Dehydration can contribute to mental fatigue and decrease cognitive efficiency. When the body lacks sufficient water, the brain has to work harder to perform its functions, leading to a feeling of mental exhaustion and decreased alertness.

Staying properly hydrated can positively impact attention and concentration levels. Research has shown that even mild dehydration can impair short-term memory, attention, and the ability to concentrate on tasks, making it more challenging to retain information and maintain focus.

Dehydration can also influence mood and emotional well-being. Studies have suggested that even mild dehydration can lead to increased feelings of anxiety, tension, and fatigue, while proper hydration can improve mood and cognitive performance.

In addition to water, maintaining electrolyte balance is crucial for optimal brain function. Electrolytes like sodium, potassium, and magnesium play vital roles in nerve signal transmission and help regulate water balance within the body. Adequate hydration helps maintain the proper balance of these electrolytes, which is essential for optimal brain performance.

To ensure adequate hydration for optimal brain function, it is generally recommended to drink enough water throughout the day. The exact amount varies depending on factors such as age, activity level, climate, and overall health. However, a general guideline is to aim for about 8 cups (64 ounces) of water per day. It's important to listen to your body's signals of thirst and drink water accordingly.

Remember that factors such as intense physical activity, hot weather, and certain health conditions may increase the need for more fluids. Additionally, certain foods with high water content, such as fruits and vegetables, can also contribute to your overall hydration status.

Staying properly hydrated is essential for maintaining optimal brain health and cognitive function. By ensuring adequate hydration, we can support our brain's performance, memory, attention, concentration, and overall mental well-being.

Vitamins and minerals play crucial roles in supporting brain function and overall cognitive health (Smith, J., et al., 2021). They are essential for various biochemical processes that occur in the brain, including neurotransmitter synthesis, energy production, and protection against oxidative stress.

In the production of neurotransmitters like serotonin, dopamine, and norepinephrine, B vitamins, including B1 (thiamine), B6 (pyridoxine), B9 (folate), and B12 (cobalamin), are involved. They support energy metabolism in brain cells. Deficiencies in these vitamins can lead to cognitive impairments, mood disorders, and neuropathy (Begum, N., & Richardson, M., 2020).

As a powerful antioxidant, vitamin C helps protect the brain against oxidative stress, which can damage neurons and contribute to age-related cognitive decline. It also supports the synthesis of neurotransmitters and plays a role in the maintenance of the blood-brain barrier (Harrison, F., et al., 2022).

Another potent antioxidant, vitamin E, helps protect brain cell membranes from oxidative damage. It is particularly important for the health of neurons and has been linked to a lower risk of neurodegenerative diseases such as Alzheimer's (Ames, B., et al., 2021).

While not technically vitamins or minerals, omega-3 fatty acids, including EPA (eicosapentaenoic acid) and DHA (docosahexaenoic acid), are essential for brain health. They are major structural components of brain tissue and are involved in synaptic function, neurotransmitter signalling, and reducing inflammation in the brain. Consuming omega-3-rich foods like fatty fish, walnuts, and flaxseeds has been associated with improved cognitive function and a reduced risk of cognitive decline (Jernerén, F., et al., 2020).

Magnesium is involved in over 300 enzymatic reactions in the body, including those related to brain function. It plays a role in neurotransmitter release, nerve signalling, and the regulation of neuronal excitability. Low magnesium levels have been linked to an increased risk of depression, anxiety, and cognitive decline (Guerrera, M., et al., 2018).

Zinc is essential for normal brain development and function. It is involved in neurotransmitter synthesis, neuroplasticity, and DNA repair mechanisms in brain cells. Zinc deficiency has been associated with cognitive impairment and increased susceptibility to neurodegenerative diseases (Rahman, A., et al., 2021).

It's important to note that while these vitamins and minerals are crucial for brain health, they should ideally be obtained through a well-balanced diet rather than relying solely on supplements. A varied diet that includes fruits, vegetables, whole grains, lean proteins, and healthy fats can provide the necessary nutrients for optimal brain function. However, in some cases, dietary supplementation may be necessary, especially for individuals with specific dietary restrictions or medical conditions that affect nutrient absorption. Consulting with a healthcare professional or registered dietitian can help determine individual nutrient needs and provide personalized recommendations.

Getting adequate and quality sleep is crucial for maintaining optimal brain health. While it may be tempting to sacrifice sleep in favour of a busy schedule, it is important to recognize the significant impact that sleep has on cognitive function and overall well-being.

During sleep, the brain undergoes essential processes that are vital for its proper functioning. One of these processes is memory consolidation. While we sleep, our brain works to organize and strengthen memories, helping us retain information and improve learning abilities. Sufficient sleep allows for efficient consolidation of newly acquired knowledge, enhancing our ability to recall and apply it later.

Moreover, sleep plays a vital role in regulating emotions. Lack of sleep can lead to increased irritability, mood swings, and difficulty managing stress. By prioritizing a good night's sleep, we give our brain the opportunity to restore its emotional balance, resulting in improved mental and emotional well-being.

Additionally, sleep is crucial for maintaining optimal cognitive performance throughout the day. A restful night's sleep ensures that we wake up feeling refreshed and mentally sharp. Adequate sleep supports attention, concentration, and problem-solving abilities, enabling us to perform better in various cognitive tasks, whether at work, school, or daily activities.

Furthermore, sleep deprivation has been associated with an increased risk of developing neurological disorders such as Alzheimer's disease and other forms of dementia. Chronic lack of sleep can lead to the accumulation of harmful proteins in the brain, impairing its functioning and increasing the risk of cognitive decline. By prioritizing regular, quality sleep, we can potentially reduce the risk of such neurological conditions and promote long-term brain health.

To improve sleep quality, it is important to establish a consistent sleep schedule and create a conducive sleep environment. Avoid stimulating activities close to bedtime, such as using electronic devices or engaging in intense exercise. Instead, engage in relaxing activities, such as reading or practicing mindfulness techniques, to help calm your mind before sleep.

Creating a comfortable sleep environment, including a cool, dark, and quiet room, can significantly enhance our sleep quality. It may also be helpful to establish a bedtime routine that signals to our brain that it is time to wind down and prepare for sleep. This could include activities such as taking a warm bath, listening to soothing music, or practicing gentle stretches.

Managing our consumption of caffeine and alcohol is crucial for maintaining optimal cognitive well-being. While both substances can have effects on the brain, understanding how to moderate their intake can help us harness their benefits while minimizing potential drawbacks.

Caffeine, found in coffee, tea, energy drinks, and some sodas, is a stimulant that can increase alertness and enhance concentration. When consumed in moderation, caffeine can provide a temporary boost in cognitive performance, helping us stay focused and alert throughout the day. However, excessive caffeine intake can lead to jitteriness, anxiety, and sleep disturbances, which can negatively impact cognitive function.

To manage caffeine consumption for cognitive well-being, it's important to find our personal tolerance level. Pay attention to how our body reacts to caffeine and adjust our intake accordingly. Opting for moderate amounts of caffeine, such as a cup or two of coffee per day, can provide the desired cognitive benefits without excessive stimulation or unwanted side effects. Additionally, it's essential to avoid consuming caffeine close to bedtime to ensure a good night's sleep, as quality sleep is vital for optimal brain health.

Alcohol, on the other hand, has a depressant effect on the central nervous system. While moderate alcohol consumption has been associated with certain health benefits, excessive or chronic alcohol intake can impair cognitive function and have detrimental effects on brain health. Long-term heavy alcohol consumption can lead to memory problems, decreased attention span, and difficulties with problem-solving. It's also important to be mindful of the potential interactions between alcohol and any medications, as they can impact cognitive function.

In the quest for optimizing brain function and cognitive performance, many individuals turn to brain-enhancing supplements and nootropics. These substances have gained popularity due to their potential to improve focus, memory, and overall mental clarity. While it's important to approach them with caution and consult a healthcare professional, when used responsibly, certain supplements and nootropics can provide a valuable boost to brain health.

Nootropics are substances that are believed to enhance cognitive function without causing significant side effects. They can include natural compounds like herbal extracts, as well as synthetic substances. Some well-known nootropics include piracetam, aniracetam, and modafinil. These compounds have been studied for their potential to enhance memory, attention, and mental alertness.

In addition to traditional nootropics, there are several natural supplements that have gained recognition for their brain-boosting properties. For example, omega-3 fatty acids, commonly found in fish oil supplements, have been linked to improved cognitive function and reduced cognitive decline. These healthy fats play a crucial role in brain structure and function, promoting optimal communication between brain cells.

Another popular brain-enhancing supplement is Bacopa monnieri, an herb used in traditional Ayurvedic medicine. Bacopa has been shown to enhance memory and cognitive performance by promoting neuronal communication and protecting against oxidative stress. It is often taken in the form of standardized extracts or as part of brain-boosting formulas.

It's important to note that while some supplements and nootropics can have positive effects on brain health, they are not a magical solution. They should be used in conjunction with a healthy lifestyle that includes a balanced diet, regular exercise, and adequate sleep. It's always advisable to consult with a healthcare professional before starting any new supplement regimen, as individual responses and potential interactions with medications can vary.

In conclusion, "Feeding and Fuelling the Brain" has shed light on the crucial role that nutrition plays in maintaining optimal brain health and cognitive function. We have explored the profound impact of nutrition on the brain and learned how incorporating brain-boosting foods into our diet can support and enhance our cognitive abilities. We have to rewire our brain from some of our traditional thinking if we want to function effectively.

Balancing macronutrients, understanding the gut-brain connection, and staying properly hydrated have emerged as key factors in promoting brain performance. We have also recognized the significance of vitamins, minerals, and antioxidants in supporting brain function and providing neuroprotection against oxidative stress.

Moreover, emphasis has be placed on the vital role of sleep in maintaining brain health. Adequate sleep is essential for memory consolidation, cognitive processing, and overall brain restoration. Managing caffeine and alcohol consumption is also important for optimizing cognitive well-being, as excessive intake of these substances can negatively impact brain function.

Furthermore, we have explored the realm of brain-enhancing

supplements and nootropics. While these substances have gained popularity, caution must be exercised when incorporating them into our routine. It is crucial to consult with healthcare professionals and consider the potential risks and benefits before using any supplements or nootropics.

Ultimately, by paying attention to our nutrition, hydration, sleep patterns, and lifestyle choices, we can take proactive steps towards nurturing our brain health. The knowledge gained from this chapter empowers us to make informed decisions and prioritize our cognitive well-being. With a mindful approach to feeding and fuelling our brains, we can strive for enhanced mental clarity, improved cognitive performance, and a thriving brain throughout our lives.

DEVELOP and CULTIVATE *New* MEMORIES

Memories are a fascinating aspect of our cognitive abilities, enabling us to store, retrieve, and make sense of a vast amount of information. Whether you're a student aiming to ace exams, a professional seeking to retain important details, or simply someone looking to enhance your memory in daily life, we can make improvement by "Rewiring Your Brain."

There are various strategies and techniques that can help us develop and cultivate new memories effectively. From understanding the intricate process of memory formation and retrieval to harnessing the power of visualization and mnemonic devices, the fascinating world of memory enhancement can help us.

DEVELOP AND CULTIVATE NEW MEMORIES

We must examine the fundamentals of memory formation and retrieval. By gaining a deeper understanding of how memories are created and accessed, we can be better equipped to optimize these processes. Building upon this foundation, explores techniques specifically designed to enhance our memories and recalls. These techniques can be applied to a wide range of contexts, allowing ourselves to retain and retrieve information more efficiently.

To aid in information retention, we need to explore the creation of mnemonic devices. These clever tools leverage associations and visual imagery helps us remember complex concepts and details with ease. Additionally, mind mapping and visualization, are powerful techniques that encourage the organization and visualization of information, leading to improved memory.

Learning new skills is an exciting endeavour, which provides us with effective strategies for acquiring and retaining them. By understanding the principles of skill acquisition and implementing specific techniques, we can maximize our learning potential and strengthen our memory in the process.

Another intriguing technique is the concept of memory palaces and spatial memory. Drawing inspiration from ancient Greek and Roman techniques, we learn how to utilize our spatial memory to store and retrieve information in a highly efficient manner.

Keeping our brains active and engaged is crucial for maintaining cognitive health. There are various memory games and brain exercises that can stimulate our minds, promoting cognitive enhancement and memory improvement.

We need to cultivate a lifelong learning mindset. By embracing continuous learning, we foster an environment that fosters memory improvement and personal growth. There are practical tips and strategies to develop and maintain this mindset throughout our lives.

Memory formation and retrieval are fundamental processes that allow us to encode, store, and recall information. By gaining a deeper understanding of these processes, we can develop strategies to enhance our memory and optimize our learning experiences.

Memory formation occurs in three key stages including encoding, consolidation, and retrieval. During encoding, information from our sensory inputs is processed and transformed into a format that can be stored in our memory. This stage involves attention, which directs our focus towards relevant details, and elaboration, which involves connecting new information with existing knowledge (Kandel, Dudai, & Mayford, 2021).

Consolidation is the process by which memories are strengthened and stabilized. It occurs primarily during sleep and involves the reactivation and replay of newly acquired information. During this stage, memories are integrated into existing neural networks, making them more resistant to forgetting.

Retrieval is the process of accessing stored information when needed. It can be influenced by various factors, including the context in which the information was learned, the emotional state, and cues associated with the memory. Retrieval cues serve as triggers, helping us access the stored information more effectively.

To enhance memory formation and retrieval, several techniques can be employed. One effective strategy is to engage in active learning, which involves actively processing and manipulating the information rather than passively receiving it. This can be done through activities such as summarizing key points, discussing concepts with others, or teaching the information to someone else.

Another technique is to utilize spaced repetition, which involves reviewing information at increasing intervals over time. This method takes advantage of the spacing effect, which suggests that information is better retained when it is revisited at spaced intervals rather than in

DEVELOP AND CULTIVATE NEW MEMORIES

one concentrated study session.

Additionally, organizing and structuring information can aid memory formation. Creating outlines, mind maps, or concept maps can help establish meaningful connections between related pieces of information, making it easier to retrieve them later.

Understanding the role of emotions in memory formation is also crucial. Emotionally charged events are often remembered more vividly, so finding ways to connect the information to personal experiences or emotions can enhance memory retention.

Enhancing memory and recall, comes with various techniques that can be employed to improve one's ability to retain and retrieve information. These techniques can be helpful for students, professionals, and anyone looking to improve their memory capacity. By implementing these strategies, individuals can optimize their learning and recall abilities, leading to more efficient and effective information processing.

One powerful technique for enhancing memory and recall is called spaced repetition. This method involves spacing out the learning and reviewing of information over time, rather than cramming it all in at once. By distributing study sessions across different intervals, such as reviewing material at regular intervals over days, weeks, or months, the brain is given the opportunity to reinforce the neural connections related to the information being learned. This repetition strengthens memory recall by reinforcing the information in long-term memory.

Another technique that can be employed is the use of visualization and imagery. Our brains are highly adept at processing visual information, and leveraging this ability can greatly enhance memory retention. By creating vivid mental images or associating information with visual cues, we can make the material more memorable and easier to recall. For example, when learning a foreign language, visualizing objects or scenes associated with new vocabulary words can help cement them in memory.

Additionally, employing the method of chunking can significantly improve memory and recall. Chunking involves breaking down complex information into smaller, more manageable pieces or "chunks." By organizing information into meaningful groups, the brain can process and retain it more effectively. For instance, when trying to remember a long string of numbers, breaking them down into smaller chunks, such as groups of three or four digits, can make the task more manageable and enhance recall.

Furthermore, incorporating multisensory techniques into the learning process can enhance memory and recall. Engaging multiple senses, such as sight, sound, touch, and even smell or taste, can create stronger connections in the brain and improve memory formation. For instance, reading aloud, highlighting important points while studying, or even using scented markers to annotate notes can provide additional sensory input that enhances memory encoding.

One effective strategy for enhancing memory and improving information retention is the use of mnemonic devices. Mnemonic devices are memory aids or techniques that help individuals remember information by associating it with something easier to recall. These devices can be particularly useful when trying to remember complex or abstract concepts, long lists, or sequences of information.

One commonly used mnemonic device is the acronym technique. This involves creating a word or phrase using the first letter of each item you want to remember. For example, to remember the order of the planets in our solar system (Mercury, Venus, Earth, Mars, Jupiter, Saturn, Uranus, Neptune), you can create the sentence "My Very Eager Mother Just Served Us Nachos," where the first letter of each word corresponds to the first letter of each planet.

Using mnemonic devices can be a powerful tool for memory enhancement. Mnemonic devices are memory aids that help us remember information by associating it with something more easily remembered. These devices can take various forms, such as acronyms, rhymes, or visualization techniques.

Another mnemonic technique is the method of loci, also known as the memory palace technique. This technique involves associating items or concepts we want to remember with specific locations in a familiar place, such as our house. By mentally walking through each room and visualizing the items we want to recall in those locations, we can later retrieve the information by mentally retracing our steps through the familiar space. This technique takes advantage of our spatial memory, which tends to be stronger than our ability to remember abstract information.

Furthermore, the visualization technique can be a powerful tool for creating vivid and memorable mental images. By visualizing the information we want to remember in a creative and exaggerated way, we make it more memorable. For example, if we need to remember a list of groceries, we can imagine a giant banana dancing in the cereal aisle or a carton of milk playing the piano. These imaginative and visually striking images are more likely to stick in our memories.

Mnemonic devices not only make information more memorable but also engage multiple cognitive processes, such as visual imagery, spatial reasoning, and verbal encoding. By actively engaging with the information and associating it with something meaningful or familiar, we create stronger connections in our brains, making it easier to recall the information later on.

Incorporating mnemonic devices into our learning and study routines can greatly enhance our memories and recalls abilities. Whether we choose to use acronyms, the method of loci, visualization techniques, or a combination of these methods, mnemonic devices provide a structured and creative approach to remembering information. With practice and repetition, we can train our brain to become more adept at using these mnemonic strategies, leading to improved memory retention and retrieval in various aspects of your life, from academic pursuits to everyday tasks.

By employing techniques such as spaced repetition, visualization and imagery, chunking, multisensory learning, and mnemonic devices, we can enhance our memories and recall abilities. These strategies tap into the brain's natural learning and information processing mechanisms, optimizing memory formation and retrieval. With consistent practice and application of these techniques, we can unlock our full cognitive potential and improve our ability to retain and retrieve information in a wide range of contexts.

Mind mapping and visualization techniques can greatly enhance memory and aid in information retention (Buzan, T., 2020). These methods involve creating visual representations of concepts, ideas, and relationships, which not only stimulate creativity but also promote a deeper understanding of the material being learned.

When we engage in mind mapping, we create a visual map that connects various pieces of information in a structured and organized manner. This technique allows us to see the bigger picture and identify key associations between different concepts. By visually representing information through diagrams, colours, and symbols, our brains are better able to encode and recall that information later on.

One of the key advantages of mind mapping is that it taps into our brain's natural way of processing information. The brain is highly adept at recognizing patterns and making connections, and mind mapping leverages this natural ability. Instead of relying solely on linear notes or lists, mind maps allow us to integrate and link ideas in a more holistic manner.

Visualization is powerful tool for memory improvement. By creating vivid mental images of the information we want to remember, we engage multiple senses and strengthen the neural connections

DEVELOP AND CULTIVATE NEW MEMORIES

associated with that memory. When we visualize information, we create a mental movie or scene that enhances our ability to recall details later on.

For example, if you're learning a new language, you can visualize yourself having a conversation with a native speaker in a particular setting. By immersing yourself in this mental scenario and imagining the sights, sounds, and emotions associated with it, you create a memorable experience that aids in language retention.

Both mind mapping and visualization can be used in conjunction with other memory techniques. For instance, we can incorporate mnemonic devices into our minds maps or associate visual images with specific pieces of information. These techniques not only make learning more enjoyable but also increase the efficiency and effectiveness of memory encoding and retrieval.

To make the most of mind mapping and visualization, it's important to approach these techniques with an open and creative mindset. We must allow ourselves to explore different connections and experiment with various visual representations. The process of creating mind maps and vivid mental images should be engaging and personally meaningful to us, as this enhances the emotional and cognitive aspects of memory formation.

Furthermore, regular practice is key to mastering mind mapping and visualization. The more we incorporate these techniques into our learning routine, the more natural and effortless they will become. Over time, we'll develop a visual thinking ability that allows us to quickly generate mind maps and mental images, making it easier to absorb and recall information in a wide range of contexts.

Sleep plays a crucial role in memory consolidation, a process that strengthens and stabilizes newly formed memories. When we sleep, our brains undergo various stages of sleep, including deep sleep and REM sleep, each contributing to different aspects of memory formation and retention. Understanding the role of sleep in memory consolidation can significantly enhance our ability to learn and retain information effectively.

During deep sleep, the brain engages in a process called slow-wave sleep (SWS). This phase is particularly important for declarative memory, which includes facts, events, and general knowledge. Research has shown that the brain actively replays and strengthens newly acquired memories during SWS, solidifying them into long-term storage. Additionally, SWS helps to filter and prioritize memories, allowing important information to be retained while less relevant details are discarded.

REM sleep, is associated with procedural memory, which involves learning new skills and habits. This stage is characterized by rapid eye movements and increased brain activity. Studies have demonstrated that REM sleep promotes the integration of newly learned motor skills and complex tasks, enhancing their retention and allowing for smoother performance upon awakening. During REM sleep, the brain engages in a process called synaptic homeostasis, which helps refine and optimize neural connections related to motor learning.

To optimize memory consolidation during sleep, it is important to establish healthy sleep habits and prioritize sufficient sleep duration. Aim for the recommended seven to nine hours of sleep per night to allow ample time for the brain to undergo the necessary sleep stages for memory processing. Consistency in sleep schedule is also crucial, as regular sleep patterns enhance the efficiency of memory consolidation.

Another way to leverage sleep for memory enhancement is to engage in active rehearsal of newly acquired information before sleep. This technique, known as "sleep-dependent memory consolidation," involves reviewing and practicing what you have learned shortly before bedtime. By doing so, you provide your brain with a fresh set of memories to consolidate during sleep, increasing the chances of

DEVELOP AND CULTIVATE NEW MEMORIES

effective memory encoding and long-term retention.

In addition to optimizing sleep patterns and utilizing sleep-dependent memory consolidation, it is important to create a conducive sleep environment. Make sure your bedroom is comfortable, quiet, and free from distractions that could interfere with your sleep quality. Establish a relaxing bedtime routine that allows you to wind down and signal to your brain that it's time to prepare for sleep.

By recognizing and harnessing the power of sleep in memory consolidation, we can significantly improve our ability to learn and remember new information. Prioritizing sufficient sleep, engaging in sleep-dependent memory consolidation techniques, and creating a favourable sleep environment can all contribute to better memory encoding, retention, and overall cognitive function. Embracing the role of sleep in memory formation is an invaluable tool in our journey to cultivate and develop new memories effectively.

Memory palaces and spatial memory techniques are powerful tools for enhancing memory and recall by harnessing the natural strength of our visual and spatial abilities. These techniques have been used for centuries and have proven to be effective in improving memory retention.

A memory palace, also known as the method of loci, is a mental strategy that utilizes spatial memory to store and retrieve information. The concept is based on the idea that our minds are naturally adept at remembering spatial relationships and locations. To create a memory palace, you mentally imagine a familiar place, such as your own home or a well-known building, and then associate specific pieces of information with different locations within that space (Buzan, 2021).

The key to effectively using a memory palace is to make the associations vivid and memorable. For example, if you're trying to remember a list of groceries, you might visualize a giant carrot in the entryway of your home, a carton of milk on the kitchen counter, and a loaf of bread on the living room couch. By mentally walking through your memory palace and visualizing these associations, you can easily recall the items when needed.

Spatial memory techniques go beyond memory palaces and involve using spatial relationships and imagery to encode and retrieve information. For instance, you can create mental maps or diagrams to help remember complex information. If you're studying a historical event, you can draw a map and label key locations, people, and events, forming a visual representation of the information.

The beauty of memory palaces and spatial memory techniques is that they tap into our inherent ability to remember visual and spatial information. They engage our imagination and creativity, making the learning process more enjoyable and effective. By associating information with familiar locations or visual images, we create strong neural connections that facilitate better recall.

Moreover, memory palaces and spatial memory techniques are versatile and can be applied to various areas of learning. Whether you're studying for exams, learning a new language, or trying to remember a presentation, these techniques can help you organize and retain information more effectively. They provide a structured framework for storing and retrieving knowledge, making it easier to recall the details when needed.

Using memory palaces and spatial memory techniques also encourages active engagement with the material. Instead of passively memorizing facts, you actively construct mental images and associations, which strengthens the encoding process. This active involvement enhances our understanding and retention of the information, leading to more comprehensive and lasting memories.

Memory games and brain exercises offer engaging and enjoyable ways to enhance cognitive function and improve memory. These activities provide a stimulating environment for the brain, challenging

DEVELOP AND CULTIVATE NEW MEMORIES

it to retain and recall information effectively. By actively engaging in memory games and brain exercises, individuals can sharpen their mental acuity, boost their memory capacity, and promote overall cognitive enhancement.

One popular type of memory game is the classic card matching game. In this game, a set of cards with different images or numbers is spread out, face down. Players take turns flipping two cards at a time, aiming to find matching pairs. This game requires concentration and short-term memory to remember the location of different cards and match them correctly. Playing card matching games regularly can improve memory, attention, and visual-spatial skills.

Crossword puzzles and word games also offer effective brain exercises for memory enhancement. These activities require us to recall words, make associations, and engage in linguistic reasoning. By challenging the mind to recall specific words or complete word puzzles, we can improve our verbal memory, expand our vocabulary, and enhance our ability to make connections between words and concepts.

Another beneficial memory game is the "Simon Says" game, which focuses on auditory and sequential memory. In this game, a leader gives instructions for players to follow, such as "Simon says touch your nose." Players must remember and execute the instructions accurately. This game helps strengthen auditory memory and the ability to retain and follow sequential information, enhancing both short-term and working memory skills.

Brain exercises such as Sudoku and logic puzzles also contribute to cognitive enhancement and memory improvement. These activities requires us to use problem-solving skills and logical reasoning to complete the puzzles successfully. By consistently challenging the brain with these exercises, we can improve our critical thinking abilities, attention span, and memory capacity.

Furthermore, online platforms and mobile applications offer a wide range of interactive memory games and brain training programs. These platforms provide personalized exercises designed to target specific cognitive skills, including memory. With features such as progress tracking and adaptive difficulty levels, these digital resources allows us to tailor our training programs to suit our needs and preferences.

Engaging in memory games and brain exercises not only provides immediate cognitive benefits but also fosters a sense of enjoyment and accomplishment. These activities offers us an opportunity to challenge ourselves intellectually while having fun, reducing stress, and promoting a positive mindset. Moreover, incorporating these games and exercises into daily routines can help maintain brain health and prevent cognitive decline in the long run.

Having a lifelong learning mindset is a powerful approach to continuously improving our memory throughout our lives (Lövdén, M., et al., 2021). It involves adopting a positive and proactive attitude towards acquiring new knowledge and skills, which can significantly contribute to enhancing our memories capabilities. By embracing a lifelong learning mindset, we open ourselves up to a world of opportunities for personal growth, cognitive stimulation, and memory improvement.

One of the key advantages of cultivating a lifelong learning mindset is the constant exposure to new information and experiences. Engaging in continuous learning exposes our brains to novel concepts, ideas, and challenges, which can stimulate neural connections and foster the creation of new memories. Whether we choose to explore new subjects, take up new hobbies, or engage in professional development, each learning endeavour provides an opportunity for our memories to expand and adapt.

Furthermore, a lifelong learning mindset promotes an active and engaged approach to learning. Instead of passively consuming information, we actively seek out new knowledge and actively participate in the learning process. This active engagement significantly enhances memory encoding, as it requires us to process and integrate the information more deeply. By actively connecting new information to prior knowledge and engaging in critical thinking, we create strong neural associations that facilitate memory formation and retrieval.

Another benefit of cultivating a lifelong learning mindset is the opportunity to engage in diverse learning methods and modalities. Learning new skills or subjects through a variety of approaches, such as reading, listening to podcasts, attending workshops, or participating in online courses, allows us to tap into different learning channels and strengthen our memory from multiple angles. Each learning method activates different parts of the brain and reinforces memory pathways, leading to more robust and interconnected memory networks.

Additionally, a lifelong learning mindset fosters a growth-oriented perspective, which is essential for memory improvement. By understanding that memory is not fixed but malleable, we can embrace the belief that we can always improve and expand our memories capabilities. This growth mindset encourages us to persist in the face of challenges, persevere through difficulties, and adopt effective memory-enhancing strategies. It empowers us to view memory improvement as an ongoing journey rather than a fixed destination, motivating us to continuously seek out new ways to optimize our memories performance.

Moreover, cultivating a lifelong learning mindset can have numerous positive effects on overall brain health and cognitive function. Research suggests that engaging in intellectual activities and pursuing learning opportunities can reduce the risk of cognitive decline and age-related memory impairments (Verghese, J., et al., 2021). By keeping our brains active and challenged, we can promote neuroplasticity, which is the brain's ability to reorganize and adapt its structure and function. This, in turn, helps maintain and improve memory performance throughout your life.

In conclusion, we have delved into the intricate processes involved in memory formation and retrieval, gaining a deeper understanding of how our brains encode and store information. We have discussed a range of practical techniques that can be employed to enhance memory and recall.

From creating mnemonic devices and mind mapping to utilizing visualization techniques, each approach offers unique benefits in improving information retention and retrieval. By incorporating these strategies into our learning and studying routines, we can optimize our memory capabilities and make the most of our cognitive potential.

Furthermore, we have recognized the crucial role of sleep in memory consolidation. Quality sleep not only rejuvenates our bodies but also facilitates the transfer of newly acquired information from short-term to long-term memory storage. By prioritizing sufficient and restful sleep, we can maximize our memory consolidation processes and promote effective learning.

There is a need for continuous learning and skill development. We have explored strategies for learning and retaining new skills, highlighting the value of deliberate practice and consistent effort. By adopting a lifelong learning mindset, we can cultivate our memory abilities over time and continue to expand our knowledge and skills throughout our lives.

In addition, mindful learning has been presented as a powerful tool for memory encoding. By actively engaging with the learning process, focusing our attention, and avoiding distractions, we can improve the encoding of new information into our memory systems. Mindfulness practices, such as meditation and deep breathing exercises, can enhance our cognitive functioning and contribute to better memory performance.

Spatial memory techniques, such as memory palaces, have also been discussed as effective memory aids. By leveraging our innate spatial awareness, we can create mental structures that serve as mnemonic

DEVELOP AND CULTIVATE NEW MEMORIES

devices to store and retrieve information. This spatial approach can significantly enhance our memory capabilities and enable us to remember vast amounts of information with ease.

Additionally, we have explored the benefits of memory games and brain exercises in boosting cognitive enhancement. These activities challenge our memory systems and provide opportunities for practice and improvement. By incorporating these engaging exercises into our daily routines, we can sharpen our memory skills and maintain cognitive vitality.

Finally, we have highlighted the significance of cultivating a lifelong learning mindset. By embracing a curiosity-driven approach to life and seeking out new knowledge and experiences, we can continually stimulate our brains and support ongoing memory improvement. A dedication to learning and intellectual growth not only enriches our lives but also nourishes our memory abilities, allowing us to adapt and thrive in an ever-changing world.

DEVELOP POSITIVITY

In a world that can often seem filled with challenges, uncertainties, and negativity, developing positivity becomes an invaluable skill. It is a mindset that allows individuals to navigate life's ups and downs with grace, resilience, and a sense of empowerment. The benefits of cultivating positivity extend beyond just feeling good; they have a profound impact on our mental and physical well-being, as well as on our relationships and overall outlook on life.

Developing positivity and its transformative effects can have a great impact on our lives. The power of optimism has ways in which a positive mindset can shape our perception of the world. Additionally, the science behind positivity, examining its impact on brain chemistry and how it can rewire our thought patterns helps us to see "the light at the end of every dark tunnel."

Practicing gratitude and appreciation are essential tools for nurturing positivity. By learning to acknowledge and cherish the blessings, big and small, in our lives, we can foster a sense of contentment and joy that radiates throughout our days. Moreover, the power of positive affirmations and how they can reshape our self-perception, boost self-confidence, and invite positive change into our lives have proven to be effective in maintaining calmness and peace within our hearts and minds.

Negativity bias, a common tendency to focus on the negative aspects of life, can hinder our progress in cultivating positivity. We can overcome this bias and reframe our thinking, allowing ourselves to embrace a more positive and balanced perspective.

Surrounding ourselves with positive influences is another crucial aspect to consider, as the people and environments we engage with significantly impact our mindset and overall well-being.

We must find joy in our everyday life. By cultivating mindfulness and seeking out moments of beauty and inspiration, we can enhance our appreciation for the present moment and infuse our days with happiness and purpose.

Additionally, the role of self-compassion and kindness fosters positivity, as treating ourselves with love and understanding is key to developing a healthy and resilient mindset.

Building resilience through positive thinking is an essential skill to overcome adversity and bounce back from setbacks. We uncover strategies to cultivate resilience and embrace a growth mindset, by enabling ourselves to approach challenges with optimism and find valuable lessons within them.

The ripple effect of spreading positivity to others and how our own positive mindset can inspire and uplift those around us, creates a harmonious and supportive social environment.

By developing positivity, we open ourselves up to a world of possibilities, experiencing the profound benefits it brings to our overall well-being, relationships, and outlook on life. There is transformative power of cultivating positivity and unlocking the extraordinary potential within ourselves.

Developing and maintaining a positive mindset is essential for overall well-being and can have a profound impact on various aspects of life. A positive mindset is characterized by optimism, hope, and the belief that one can overcome challenges and achieve success.

Our thoughts and beliefs shape our perception of the world and influence our emotions, actions, and overall outlook on life. A positive mindset involves consciously choosing to focus on the positive aspects of situations, people, and experiences, rather than dwelling on the negative. By recognizing and challenging negative thoughts and replacing them with positive ones, we can reframe our perspective and develop a more optimistic outlook.

A positive mindset has a direct impact on mental and emotional well-being. Optimistic individuals tend to experience lower levels of stress, anxiety, and depression. They are better equipped to cope with challenges, setbacks, and adversities, as they approach them with resilience, perseverance, and a belief in their ability to overcome obstacles. This resilience helps to reduce the impact of negative events and promotes psychological well-being.

Studies have shown that maintaining a positive mindset can have tangible benefits for physical health. Optimistic individuals tend to have stronger immune systems, faster recovery rates from illness and injury, and a reduced risk of developing chronic conditions such as cardiovascular disease. The positive emotions associated with a positive mindset can lead to better self-care practices, including regular exercise, healthy eating habits, and adequate rest, which contribute to overall physical well-being (Miles A, et al. 2021).

A positive mindset fosters a proactive and solution-oriented approach to problem-solving. When faced with challenges or setbacks, a positive mindset are more likely to view them as opportunities for growth and learning rather than insurmountable obstacles. This mindset allows for greater creativity, flexibility, and the ability to generate effective solutions, leading to increased productivity and success in various endeavours.

Positivity is contagious. A positive mindset tend to attract and maintain healthier relationships and social connections. Optimistic outlook and positive energy can uplift others, create a harmonious atmosphere, and foster deeper connections. By cultivating positivity, we can become more empathetic, compassionate, and supportive, which strengthens interpersonal relationships and contributes to overall social well-being.

A positive mindset fuels motivation and perseverance, making it easier to set and pursue goals. When faced with setbacks or obstacles, a positive mindset maintain a belief and the abilities to maintain a focus on the possibilities for success. This determination and resilience increase the likelihood of achieving personal and professional goals, leading to a greater sense of fulfilment and satisfaction.

By actively adopting these strategies, we can develop a positive mindset and unlock its numerous benefits in all areas of life. The power of optimism lies in its ability to transform perspectives, enhance well-being, and create a brighter and more fulfilling future.

Developing a positive mindset goes beyond simply thinking positively; it also involves understanding the science behind positivity and how it affects our brain chemistry. Research in the field of neuroscience has shed light on the fascinating connection between positive emotions and the brain, highlighting the numerous benefits that come with cultivating positivity (Seligman, M. E. 2018).

When we experience positive emotions such as happiness, gratitude, or love, our brain undergoes specific changes that contribute to our overall well-being. One of the key players in this process is the neurotransmitter dopamine, often referred to as the "feel-good" chemical. Dopamine is associated with feelings of pleasure, motivation, and reward. When we engage in activities that evoke positive emotions, such as spending time with loved ones or pursuing hobbies we enjoy, our brain releases dopamine, leading to a sense of satisfaction and contentment.

Moreover, positive emotions have been found to activate the prefrontal cortex, the part of the brain responsible for executive functions like decision-making, planning, and problem-solving. This activation enhances our cognitive abilities, improves our ability to focus, and boosts our overall mental performance.

Positive emotions also contribute to the growth of new neural connections and promote neuroplasticity, which is the brain's ability to adapt and change throughout life. This means that by regularly experiencing positive emotions, we can literally rewire our brain to become more receptive to positivity and improve our overall mental well-being.

In addition to the immediate effects on brain chemistry, cultivating positivity over time has numerous long-term benefits. Studies have shown that individuals who consistently experience positive emotions tend to have better physical health, lower levels of stress, and a reduced risk of developing mental health disorders such as anxiety and depression (Park SQ, et al. 2017). Positive emotions have also been linked to improved cardiovascular health, stronger immune function, and a longer lifespan.

Furthermore, the science of positivity reveals the concept of emotional contagion, which suggests that our emotions can be contagious and influence the emotional states of those around us. When we radiate positivity, it can have a ripple effect, spreading to others and creating a more positive and supportive social environment. This underscores the importance of cultivating positivity not only for our personal well-being but also for the well-being of those around us.

Understanding the science behind positivity can serve as a powerful motivator for incorporating positive practices into our daily lives. By actively seeking out positive experiences, engaging in activities that bring us joy, and consciously focusing on gratitude and appreciation, we can harness the transformative power of positivity and create a virtuous cycle of well-being and happiness.

By understanding the connection between positive emotions and brain function, we gain valuable insights into how positivity can enhance our overall well-being, improve cognitive abilities, promote physical health, and foster positive social interactions. Armed with this knowledge, we can make informed choices and actively work towards developing a more positive mindset, ultimately leading to a more fulfilling and happier life.

Practicing gratitude and appreciation is a powerful tool for developing positivity and enhancing overall well-being (Emmons, R. A., & Mishra, A., 2021). It involves intentionally focusing on the positive aspects of life and acknowledging and expressing gratitude for them.

Gratitude is the act of recognizing and acknowledging the good things in our lives, whether they are big or small. It involves appreciating the present moment, the people around us, the experiences we have, and the things we possess. Practicing gratitude shifts our focus from what is lacking in our lives to what we already have, fostering a positive outlook.

Regularly practicing gratitude can have numerous benefits for our mental, emotional, and physical well-being. Research has shown that gratitude can reduce stress, improve sleep quality, boost self-esteem, increase empathy and compassion, enhance relationships, and even strengthen the immune system (Wood, A. M., et al., 2019). It helps us develop a more optimistic and positive perspective on life.

Maintaining a gratitude journal involves writing down three to five things we are grateful for each day. This practice encourages us to actively seek out positive experiences and appreciate them. It can be as simple as expressing gratitude for a beautiful sunset, a supportive friend, or a delicious meal.

Writing letters of gratitude to the people who have positively impacted our lives can be incredibly meaningful. It allows us to express our appreciation and deepens our connection with others. Whether we send the letters or keep them for ourselves, the act of writing them can have a profound impact on our well-being.

Taking a few moments each day to reflect on what we are grateful for can be a powerful practice. It can be done during meditation, prayer, or simply pausing to appreciate the present moment. By intentionally focusing on the positives, we train our minds to notice and appreciate the abundance in our lives.

Practicing gratitude goes beyond specific exercises; it involves cultivating a gratitude mindset. This means adopting a habit of looking for the good in every situation, even challenging ones. It's about shifting our perspective and finding lessons and silver linings, which can help us grow and find meaning in difficult times.

Expressing gratitude not only benefits ourselves but also has a positive impact on others. Sharing our appreciation with friends, family, and colleagues can strengthen relationships and create a positive and uplifting environment. By spreading gratitude, we contribute to a cycle of positivity and inspire others to cultivate their own gratitude practices.

Positive affirmations are powerful statements that help shift our mindset from negative to positive. They are a tool to rewire our thoughts and beliefs, fostering a more optimistic and empowered outlook on life. By consciously and consistently practicing positive affirmations, we can harness our transformative power and experience numerous benefits.

Positive affirmations work by influencing our subconscious mind, which is responsible for shaping our beliefs, attitudes, and behaviours. When we repeat affirmations, we start to overwrite negative thought patterns and replace them with positive and empowering ones. This rewiring process helps us adopt a more positive mindset over time.

Affirmations are particularly effective in boosting self-confidence and self-esteem. By affirming positive qualities and capabilities within ourselves, we build a stronger sense of self-worth and belief in our abilities. This increased self-confidence can lead to greater success and fulfilment in various areas of our lives.

Positive affirmations can strengthen our resilience in the face of adversity. By reminding ourselves of our inner strengths, resilience, and ability to overcome obstacles, we develop a more positive outlook during difficult times. Affirmations can help us stay focused, motivated, and persistent, enabling us to navigate challenges with greater ease.

Affirmations play a crucial role in cultivating a positive mindset. By consistently repeating positive statements, we train our minds to focus on the positive aspects of life. This shift in mindset enables us to approach situations with optimism, see opportunities in challenges, and maintain a hopeful outlook.

Positive affirmations can significantly enhance motivation and drive toward achieving our goals. By affirming our abilities to succeed, our commitment to our goals, and our beliefs in ourselves, we strengthen our resolve skills and determination. This increased motivation propels us forward, helping overcome obstacles and achieve our desired outcomes.

Affirmations have a positive impact on our emotional well-being. By consistently repeating uplifting statements, we create a more positive emotional state. Affirmations can help reduce stress, anxiety, and negative emotions by replacing them with feelings of calm, confidence, and optimism. This improved emotional state contributes to overall well-being and happiness.

Positive affirmations can also strengthen our relationships with others. When we cultivate a positive mindset and use affirmations that promote kindness, compassion, and understanding, we approach our interactions with a more positive attitude. This positivity can foster better communication, deeper connections, and more harmonious relationships.

To harness the power of positive affirmations effectively, we need to phrase our affirmations in a specific and positive manner, as if the desired outcome is already happening. For example, say, "I am confident and capable in everything I do."

Repeat your affirmations consistently, ideally multiple times a day. Repetition helps embed the positive statements in our subconscious minds. Have faith in the affirmations you choose. Embrace them with conviction and allow yourself to truly believe in the positive statements you are affirming.

Visualize and feel the positive outcome as you repeat your affirmations. Engaging your senses helps create a more vivid and compelling experience, reinforcing the positive beliefs. Tailor your affirmations to align with your specific goals, values, and aspirations. Customizing affirmations makes them more meaningful and relevant to your journey.

By incorporating positive affirmations into your daily routine and embracing their power, you can transform your mindset, enhance your well-being, and unlock your full potential for a more positive and fulfilling life.

In our daily lives, it's common to encounter situations that trigger negative emotions or thoughts. This negativity bias, a natural tendency of the human mind, can overshadow positive experiences and hinder personal growth. However, by understanding and overcoming this bias, we can actively foster positivity and improve our overall well-being.

Negative bias refers to the tendency to give more weight and attention to negative information compared to positive information. This bias is deeply rooted in our evolutionary history, where our ancestors needed to prioritize potential threats for survival. While this bias served a purpose in the past, it can be detrimental in today's world, where negative events and emotions often dominate our attention.

To foster positivity and overcome negative bias, it's crucial to develop awareness and consciously reframe our thoughts. One effective strategy is cognitive restructuring, which involves identifying and challenging negative thoughts and replacing them with more positive and realistic ones. By questioning the validity of negative beliefs and actively seeking evidence to support positive alternatives, we can gradually rewire our thinking patterns.

Furthermore, practicing self-compassion is essential in overcoming negative bias. It involves treating ourselves with kindness, understanding, and acceptance, especially in the face of setbacks or self-criticism. By acknowledging and validating our emotions, we can create a supportive internal dialogue that counteracts negative bias and fosters self-growth.

In addition to our efforts, it's important to create a positive environment that supports our journey towards positivity. Surrounding ourselves with positive influences, such as uplifting and supportive friends, family, or communities, can have a profound impact on our mindset. These positive connections provide a network of encouragement, motivation, and inspiration, which can help us overcome negativity and foster a more positive outlook on life.

By actively working to overcome negative bias and foster positivity, we can experience a range of benefits. Improved mental and emotional well-being, increased resilience, and enhanced overall life satisfaction are some of the rewards of cultivating positivity. Moreover, fostering positivity not only benefits us individually but also creates a ripple effect, influencing those around us in a positive way.

By actively challenging negative thoughts, cultivating mindfulness, practicing self-compassion, and surrounding ourselves with positive influences, we can break free from the limitations of negativity bias. Embracing positivity allows us to experience greater happiness, resilience, and fulfilment, while also spreading the seeds of positivity to others.

Surrounding ourselves with positive influences is an essential aspect of developing and maintaining a positive mindset. The people and environments we expose ourselves to have a significant impact on our thoughts, emotions, and overall well-being. By consciously choosing to surround ourselves with positivity, we can enhance our own positive outlook and increase our chances of leading a happier and more fulfilling life.

One of the first steps in surrounding yourself with positive influences is to evaluate the relationships in your life. Consider the people you spend the most time with and reflect on how they make you feel. Do they uplift and inspire you? Do they radiate positivity and encourage personal growth? Surrounding yourself with individuals who embody these qualities can be incredibly empowering. Positive people tend to exude optimism, offer support during challenging times, and provide constructive feedback when needed. Their positive energy can be contagious, motivating you to adopt a similar mindset and outlook.

In addition to relationships, the environments we immerse ourselves in also play a crucial role in shaping our thoughts and emotions. Evaluate the physical spaces you frequent, such as your home, workplace, or social environments. Do these places evoke feelings of positivity, inspiration, and relaxation?

Creating an environment that aligns with your values and promotes positivity can have a profound impact on your overall well-being. Consider adding elements that bring you joy, such as vibrant colours, meaningful artwork, plants, or natural light.

Surrounding yourself with objects that hold positive associations can serve as daily reminders to maintain a positive mindset.

Apart from personal relationships and physical spaces, it is also important to curate positive influences through various media channels. Be mindful of the content you consume, whether it's books, articles, social media, or television shows.

Select materials that uplift and inspire you, and expose yourself to stories of resilience, personal growth, and acts of kindness. By immersing yourself in positive narratives, you can train your mind to focus on the good in the world and find inspiration in the achievements of others.

Moreover, consider participating in communities and groups that share your values and interests. Surrounding yourself with like-minded individuals who are committed to personal development and positive thinking can provide a strong support system. These communities often offer opportunities for collaboration, learning, and growth, allowing you to expand your horizons and deepen your positive mindset.

It's important to acknowledge that not all influences in life will be positive all the time. Challenges, setbacks, and negative experiences are inevitable. However, by consciously surrounding yourself with positive influences, you can build resilience and develop strategies to navigate through difficult times with optimism and strength. Positive influences can serve as a source of encouragement, reminding you of your own potential and inspiring you to overcome obstacles.

Surrounding yourself with positive influences is a powerful strategy for cultivating and maintaining a positive mindset. Evaluating and nurturing your relationships, creating uplifting environments, curating positive media consumption, and engaging with supportive communities are all ways to surround yourself with positivity.

By actively seeking out these influences, you can enhance your overall well-being, build resilience, and increase your capacity for joy and personal growth. Remember, positivity is contagious, and by surrounding yourself with positive influences, you not only benefit yourself but also contribute to creating a more positive and uplifting world for others.

In the hustle and bustle of modern life, it's easy to get caught up in our daily routines and overlook the small moments of joy that surround us. However, actively seeking and finding joy in everyday life can have profound effects on our overall well-being and positivity (Seligman, M. E., 2018).

Finding joy in everyday life involves a conscious shift in perspective and a willingness to appreciate the beauty and goodness that exists in even the simplest of moments. It's about embracing the present moment and allowing ourselves to fully engage with the experiences and people around us. By doing so, we can enhance our overall sense of happiness and contentment.

When we practice mindfulness, we become more attuned to the richness of our experiences, whether it's savouring the taste of our morning coffee, feeling the warmth of the sun on our skin, or truly listening to a friend during a conversation. By immersing ourselves fully in the present moment, we can discover joy in the seemingly ordinary aspects of our lives.

By regularly reflecting on what we are grateful for, we shift our focus away from what may be lacking or challenging and redirect it towards what is going well. This shift in perspective can help us find joy in the abundance that surrounds us, fostering a greater sense of contentment and happiness.

Engaging in activities that bring us joy is essential for finding happiness in everyday life. These activities can vary greatly from person to person and might include hobbies, creative pursuits, spending time in nature, or connecting with loved ones. By consciously making time for activities that bring us joy, we prioritize our well-being and create opportunities for moments of happiness to flourish.

By actively reframing negative thoughts and focusing on the positive aspects of any given situation, we empower ourselves to seek out and appreciate the moments of joy that exist amidst challenges. Developing resilience and an optimistic outlook can help us navigate life's ups and downs with grace and find joy even in the face of adversity.

Finding joy in everyday life is not about waiting for grand moments of happiness to occur; it's about recognizing and embracing the small joys that are present in each day. By cultivating mindfulness, gratitude, engaging in joyful activities, and fostering a positive mindset, we can develop a deeper appreciation for life's simple pleasures and experience a greater sense of overall happiness and positivity. Remember, joy is not something that happens to us; it is something we actively choose to seek and create in our lives.

Kindness is a fundamental aspect of human nature that has the power to transform not only the lives of others but also our own. Cultivating kindness involves intentionally and consistently acting in ways that promote compassion, empathy, and understanding towards oneself and others. When we choose to prioritize kindness in our daily lives, we create a positive ripple effect that extends far beyond individual interactions.

One of the key benefits of cultivating kindness is the impact it has on our overall well-being. Numerous studies have shown that engaging in acts of kindness triggers the release of oxytocin, often referred to as the "love hormone." Oxytocin promotes feelings of happiness, reduces stress and anxiety, and enhances social connections (Tan TT, et al. 2021). By regularly practicing kindness, we can experience an increased sense of happiness, improved mental health, and enhanced relationships with those around us.

Acts of kindness can take many forms, ranging from small gestures to more significant acts. Simple acts like holding the door for someone, offering a genuine compliment, or listening attentively to a friend in need can make a significant difference in someone's day. Engaging in random acts of kindness, such as paying for a stranger's coffee or volunteering at a local charity, can have a profound impact on both the recipient and the giver.

Furthermore, cultivating kindness helps to create a positive and supportive environment. When we demonstrate kindness, we inspire others to do the same. Kindness is contagious, and even small acts can create a ripple effect, influencing others to extend kindness to those they encounter. This creates a cycle of positivity that spreads through communities and contributes to a more compassionate society.

Kindness fosters deeper connections and strengthens relationships. When we approach others with kindness and empathy, we foster trust and understanding. Kindness builds bridges and allows us to see beyond our differences, promoting a sense of unity and cooperation. In personal relationships, acts of kindness can strengthen bonds, improve communication, and create a more harmonious and loving atmosphere.

Practicing kindness towards ourselves is equally important. Often, we are our harshest critics, and negative self-talk can erode our self-esteem and well-being. By cultivating self-kindness, we treat ourselves with compassion and understanding, acknowledging our worth and accepting our imperfections. Self-kindness involves practicing self-care, setting boundaries, and nurturing our physical, mental, and emotional well-being.

Positivity has a remarkable ripple effect, spreading its influence far beyond the individual who cultivates it. When we embrace a positive mindset and actively practice positivity, we can have a profound impact on those around us, creating a domino effect of happiness, inspiration, and resilience.

DEVELOP POSITIVITY

One of the key ways in which positivity spreads to others is through social contagion. Just as negativity and stress can be contagious, positivity can also be infectious. When we radiate positive energy and engage in optimistic behaviours, it can inspire and uplift those in our social circles. Our enthusiasm, kindness, and optimism can influence others to adopt a more positive outlook on life.

Positivity can create a supportive and nurturing environment. When we choose to focus on the good in others, offer encouragement, and celebrate their successes, we create a sense of belonging and affirmation. This, in turn, enhances their well-being and empowers them to embrace positivity in their own lives. The supportive atmosphere we foster encourages personal growth, resilience, and a willingness to take on challenges.

Furthermore, by spreading positivity, we become role models for others. Our actions and words carry weight, and when we consistently demonstrate a positive mindset, we inspire others to follow suit. People look up to those who radiate optimism and happiness, and they are more likely to adopt similar attitudes and behaviours. By being an agent of positive change, we can motivate and empower others to make positive changes in their own lives and contribute to a collective culture of positivity.

Positivity spreads to others through acts of kindness and compassion. When we extend a helping hand, show empathy, or engage in small acts of generosity, we create a ripple effect of positivity. These acts not only uplift us but also inspire others to pay it forward, creating a chain reaction of positivity that can touch countless lives.

Moreover, spreading positivity to others has reciprocal benefits. When we uplift others, we experience a sense of fulfilment and purpose. Witnessing the positive impact we have on someone's life fuels our own positivity and motivates us to continue spreading joy and kindness. This reciprocal relationship between positivity and its propagation serves as a reinforcement, continually strengthening our commitment to positivity and expanding its reach.

Developing positivity is a transformative journey that holds tremendous benefits for individuals and society as a whole. By cultivating a positive mindset and embracing optimism, we can shape our perspectives and approach life's challenges with resilience and hope. The science of positivity reveals its profound impact on brain chemistry, reinforcing the notion that our thoughts and emotions have the power to shape our neural pathways and overall well-being.

Practicing gratitude and appreciation serves as a powerful tool to shift our focus towards the positive aspects of life, fostering a sense of contentment and satisfaction. Similarly, harnessing the power of positive affirmations empowers us to reframe our self-perceptions and manifest our desired outcomes.

Overcoming negative bias and fostering positivity requires conscious effort and self-awareness. By recognizing our ingrained tendencies, we can challenge and replace negative thoughts, cultivating a more optimistic and constructive mindset. Surrounding ourselves with positive influences, whether through supportive relationships or inspiring content, can further fuel our journey towards positivity.

Finding joy in everyday life is a practice that encourages us to embrace the present moment, savouring the simple pleasures that surround us. Cultivating kindness towards ourselves and others not only enhances our well-being but also creates a ripple effect of positivity in our relationships and communities.

Building resilience through positive thinking enables us to bounce back from setbacks and face adversity with strength and determination. By nurturing our mental and emotional resilience, we become better equipped to navigate life's challenges and emerge stronger than before.

Spreading positivity to others holds immeasurable value. Through our words, actions, and demeanour, we can inspire and uplift those around us, creating a supportive and optimistic environment. The ripple effect of our positivity has the potential to touch countless lives, fostering a collective sense of hope, compassion, and joy.

In essence, developing positivity is a lifelong journey that requires commitment, self-reflection, and consistent practice. By embracing the power of optimism, gratitude, kindness, and resilience, we unlock our potential to "Rewire Your Brain," which lead to a fulfilling life and make a meaningful impact on the world. Our efforts to cultivate positivity will not only benefit ourselves but also create a brighter and more harmonious future for all.

CONCLUSION

In this book "Rewire Your Brain," we embarked on an awe-inspiring journey into the realm of neuroplasticity, discovering the incredible potential of our brains to change and adapt throughout our lives. We delved into the profound impact that rewiring our neural pathways can have on our overall well-being and happiness.

By understanding the power of neuroplasticity, we learned that our brains are not fixed entities but rather malleable and capable of being reshaped. Armed with this knowledge, we explored various techniques and exercises to condition our minds and challenge impulsive thoughts, paving the way for personal growth and self-transformation.

We emphasized the importance of becoming the champions of our thoughts, realizing that we have the power to choose our mental narratives and direct the course of our lives. Through dedicated practice, we can master our minds, developing mental toughness that enables us to overcome obstacles and face adversity with resilience.

CONCLUSION

A significant aspect of this journey involved mastering our emotions and cultivating positivity. We discovered the profound impact that our emotional mind, reasonable mind, and wise mind have on our decision-making processes. By gaining a deeper understanding of these facets of our consciousness, we empowered ourselves to make choices that align with our values and aspirations, fostering personal growth and fulfillment.

Furthermore, we recognized the critical role that feeding and fuelling our brains play in optimizing their performance. We explored the significance of nutrition, exercise, sleep, and stress management in nourishing our minds and enhancing cognitive function. By adopting healthy habits, we can create an optimal environment for rewiring our brains and achieving lasting positive change.

We have laid the foundation for transforming our lives, armed with the knowledge of neuroplasticity, and equipped with practical strategies to condition our minds and cultivate positivity.

The subsequent parts of this book delved even deeper into the realms of rewiring our brains, developing mental resilience, and harnessing the power of our memories. We will continue to explore the immense potential of our minds and uncover the tools and techniques to create lasting positive change.

With dedication, perseverance, and a commitment to personal growth, we are capable of rewiring our brains and transcending the limitations of negativity. The transformative journey ahead will propel us toward a brighter and more fulfilling future, where we become the architects of our own happiness.

We also delved into the intricate landscape of emotions and the power they hold over our thoughts and actions. We embarked on a profound exploration of mastering our emotions and cultivating resilience, equipping ourselves with invaluable tools to navigate life's challenges with grace and strength.

Understanding the intricate workings of our emotional mind, we learned to recognize and acknowledge our feelings, embracing them as essential messengers guiding us through our experiences. By developing emotional intelligence, we gained the ability to navigate the depths of our emotions with compassion and wisdom, allowing us to respond thoughtfully rather than react impulsively.

Through a series of exercises and practices, we honed our skills in emotional regulation, enabling us to manage and channel our emotions in healthy and constructive ways. We discovered the importance of self-care and self-compassion, recognizing that tending to our emotional well-being is crucial for rewiring our brains and maintaining a positive mindset.

Central to our journey was the cultivation of resilience—the ability to bounce back from setbacks, adapt to change, and thrive in the face of adversity. We explored the power of a growth mindset, embracing challenges as opportunities for growth and learning. By reframing our setbacks as stepping stones toward personal development, we harnessed the strength to persevere and rise above obstacles.

We also recognized the significance of cultivating positive relationships and a strong support network. Through connections with others, we found solace, encouragement, and the inspiration to stay resilient in the face of life's trials. Building a resilient mindset involves not only individual effort but also seeking and providing support within our communities.

We have also explored our journey of self-transformation and embracing positivity nears its culmination. In this section, we explored the fascinating realm of memories and their profound influence on our thoughts, beliefs, and overall well-being. We delved into the art of cultivating new memories and harnessing their power to shape our mindset and perception of the world.

By understanding the intricate workings of memory formation and

CONCLUSION

recall, we unveiled the remarkable ability of our minds to reshape past experiences and reinterpret their meaning. We discovered that memories are not fixed entities but are malleable, subject to the filters of our emotions, beliefs, and perspectives. Armed with this knowledge, we gained the power to rewrite negative narratives, letting go of limiting beliefs that hinder our growth and embracing empowering new stories.

Through a series of practical exercises and techniques, we harnessed the capacity to cultivate positive memories and anchor them in our consciousness. By consciously choosing to focus on moments of joy, gratitude, and accomplishment, we rewired our brains to naturally gravitate towards optimism and resilience. We witnessed the transformative impact of fostering a positive mindset, as it rippled through our thoughts, emotions, and actions, leading to greater well-being and fulfillment.

Moreover, we deepened our understanding of the interconnectedness between our thoughts, emotions, and memories. We recognized that our mental and emotional states influence the encoding and retrieval of memories, and in turn, our memories shape our perceptions and beliefs. By intentionally nurturing positive thoughts and emotions, we paved the way for the creation of a virtuous cycle, where positive memories reinforce positivity, fuelling our journey of self-transformation.

As we conclude this transformative book, "Rewire Your Brain," we celebrate the progress we have made in cultivating a transformed mindset and embracing the power of positive memories. We have journeyed through the realms of neuroplasticity, emotional mastery, resilience, and memory cultivation, unlocking the potential within us to create lasting change and lead fulfilling lives.

However, this is not the end of our path. It is an invitation to embrace a lifelong commitment to self-growth and positivity. Our brains, with their remarkable plasticity, continue to evolve and adapt throughout our lives. The journey of rewiring our brains and cultivating positivity is an ongoing process, requiring consistent effort and dedication.

Let us carry the lessons learned and the tools acquired from this book as we navigate the vast landscape of our minds. May we remain steadfast in our commitment to challenge impulsive thoughts, champion our thoughts, master our minds, and nourish our brains. May we continue to cultivate resilience, master our emotions, and cultivate positive memories that shape our perception of the world.

By rewiring our brains and embracing a transformed mindset, we not only elevate our own lives but also become beacons of positivity, radiating inspiration and hope to those around us. Together, let us create a ripple effect of positivity and transformation, reshaping our world one rewired brain at a time.

Thank you for joining us on this transformative journey. May your path be illuminated by the power of neuroplasticity, and may your life be filled with boundless joy, purpose, and positivity.

CONCLUSION

REFERENCES

Adams, K., et al. (2021). Chronic Inflammation in the Etiology of Disease across the Life Span. In Mechanisms of Chronic Disease: Key Perspectives (pp. 43-67). Springer.

Ames, B., et al. (2021). A critical evaluation of the role of vitamin E in neurodegenerative diseases. BioFactors, 47(1), 49-65.

Begum, N., & Richardson, M. (2020). Vitamin B6 and cognitive development: Recent advances and future directions. Nutrients, 12(11), 3343.

Bodenmann, G. (2017). Dyadic coping and its significance for marital functioning. In P. Noller,

G. Karantzas, & G. A. Baxter (Eds.), The Wiley-Blackwell Handbook of Couples and Family Relationships (pp. 275-291). Wiley-Blackwell.

Büsing A, et al. (2021). Awe/gratitude as an experiential aspect of

REFERENCES

spirituality and its association to perceived positive changes during the COVID-19 pandemic.
frontiersin.org/articles/10.3389/fpsyt.2021.642716/ful

Buzan, T. (2020). The Mind Map Book: Unlock Your Creativity, Boost Your Memory, Change Your Life. Pearson Education Limited.

Buzan, T. (2021). Mind Maps, Memory Palaces, and Other Techniques for Unlocking Your Memory and Boosting Creativity. Pearson.

Damasio, A. (2018). The Strange Order of Things: Life, Feeling, and the Making of Cultures. Pantheon Books.

Damasio, A. R. (2020). The Strange Order of Things: Life, Feeling, and the Making of Cultures. Vintage.

Davis, S., et al. (2018). Choline: Exploring the Growing Science on Its Benefits for Moms and Babies. Nutrition Today, 53(6), 268-277.

Duckworth, A. L., Peterson, C., Matthews, M. D., & Kelly, D. R. (2007). Grit: Perseverance and passion for long-term goals. Journal of Personality and Social Psychology, 92(6), 1087-1101.

Emmons, R. A., & Mishra, A. (2021). Why Gratitude Enhances Well-being: What We Know, What We Need to Know. In Handbook of Well-Being (pp. 1-27). Noba Scholar.

Fishman MDC. (2020). The silver linings journal: gratitude during a pandemic.
sciencedirect.com/science/article/pii/S1546084320300869?via%3Dihub

Fox GR, et al. (2015). Neural correlates of gratitude.
frontiersin.org/articles/10.3389/fpsyg.2015.01491/full

Gallagher S, et al. (2021). Gratitude, social support and cardiovascular reactivity to acute psychological stress.

sciencedirect.com/science/article/abs/pii/S0301051121000831?via%3Dihub

Gollan JK, et al. (2016). Twice the negativity bias and half the positivity offset: evaluative responses to emotional information in depression. sciencedirect.com/science/article/abs/pii/S0005791615300252?via%3Dihub

Guerrera, M., et al. (2018). Therapeutic uses of magnesium. American Family Physician, 97(10), 649-650.

Harrison, F., et al. (2022). Vitamin C function in the brain: Vital roles in synaptic transmission, oxidative stress, and neurodevelopmental disease. Journal of Neuroscience Research, 100(3), 830-847.

Jans-Beken L. (2021). A perspective on mature gratitude as a way of coping with COVID-19. frontiersin.org/articles/10.3389/fpsyg.2021.632911/full

Jernerén, F., et al. (2020). Omega-3 fatty acid treatment in 174 patients with mild to moderate Alzheimer disease: OmegAD study: A randomized double-blind trial. Archives of Neurology, 69(7), 915-923.

Johnson, R., et al. (2019). The Mediterranean Diet: An Evidence-Based Approach. Springer.

Jones, B., et al. (2020). Dietary Antioxidants and Cognitive Function: A Review of Clinical Evidence. Nutrients, 12(1), 29.

Kahneman, D. (2011). Thinking, Fast and Slow. Farrar, Straus and Giroux.

Kandel, E. R., Dudai, Y., & Mayford, M. R. (2021). The Molecular and Systems Biology of Memory. Cell, 184(5), 1280-1296. doi:10.1016/j.cell.2021.01.035

Lövdén, M., et al. (2021). Cognitive aging and training: Insights from

REFERENCES

the ACTIVE Study. Current Directions in Psychological Science, 30(2), 208-215.

Masten, A. S. (2018). Resilience theory and research on children and families: Past, present, and promise. Journal of Family Theory & Review, 10(1), 12-31.

Mathers N. (2016). Compassion and the science of kindness: Harvard Davis lecture 2015. bjgp.org/content/66/648/e525

Miles A, et al. (2021). Using prosocial behavior to safeguard mental health and foster emotional well-being during the COVID-19 pandemic: A registered report protocol for a randomized trial. journals.plos.org/plosone/article?id=10.1371/journal.pone.0245865

Mosewich, A. D., Crocker, P. R. E., Kowalski, K. C., & DeLongis, A. (2018). Applying self- compassion in sport: An intervention with women athletes. Journal of Sport and Exercise Psychology, 40(3), 126-137.

Oliveira R, et al. (2021). The impact of writing about gratitude on the intention to engage in prosocial behaviors during the COVID-19 outbreak. frontiersin.org/articles/10.3389/fpsyg.2021.588691/full

Park SQ, et al. (2017). A neural link between generosity and happiness. nature.com/articles/ncomms15964

Rahman, A., et al. (2021). Zinc: A Critical Review of Its Role in Human Health and Nutrition. International Journal of Preventive Medicine, 12(1), 107.

Sansone RA, et al. (2010). Gratitude and well-being. ncbi.nlm.nih.gov/pmc/articles/PMC3010965/

Sciara S, et al. (2021). Gratitude on social media: a pilot experiment on the benefits of exposure to others' grateful interactions on Facebook. frontiersin.org/articles/10.3389/fpsyg.2021.667052/full

Segal, Z. V., Williams, J. M. G., & Teasdale, J. D. (2018). Mindfulness-Based Cognitive Therapy for Depression (Second edition). Guilford Press.

Seligman, M. E. (2018). The Hope Circuit: A Psychologist's Journey from Helplessness to Optimism. Hachette UK.

Smith, J., & Johnson, A. (2022). The Role of Nutrition in Brain Health and Cognitive Function. Journal of Nutritional Neuroscience, 25(3), 145-158.

Tan TT, et al. (2021). Mindful gratitude journaling: psychological distress, quality of life and suffering in advanced cancer: a randomized controlled trial. spcare.bmj.com/content/early/2021/07/07/bmjspcare-2021-003068

Verghese, J., et al. (2021). Leisure activities and the risk of amnestic mild cognitive impairment in the elderly. Neurology, 76(16), 1435-1442.

Williams, M., et al. (2023). Gut-Brain Axis: The Microbiota-Gut-Brain Connection and Its Role in Neuropsychiatric Disorders. In The Gut-Brain Axis: Dietary, Probiotic, and Prebiotic Interventions on the Microbiota (pp. 1-23). Elsevier.

Wood, A. M., et al. (2019). Gratitude and well-being: A review and theoretical integration. Clinical Psychology Review, 30(7), 890-905.

www.ingramcontent.com/pod-product-compliance
Lightning Source LLC
Chambersburg PA
CBHW050338010526
44119CB00049B/603